A BEGINNER'S GUIDE TO CHURCH HISTORY

An overview of the Christian era from an evangelical perspective

Philip Parsons

DayOne

© Day One Publications 2019
Reprinted 2020
Reprinted 2021

ISBN 978-1-84625-642-4

British Library Cataloguing in Publication Data available

Published by Day One Publications
Ryelands Road, Leominster, HR6 8NZ
Telephone 01568 613 740
Toll Free 888 329 6630 (North Americal)
email—sales@dayone.co.uk
web site—www.dayone.co.uk

All rights reserved
No part of this publication may be reproduced, or stored in a retrieval system, or transmitted, in any form or by any means, mechanical, electronic, photocopying, recording or otherwise, without the prior permission of Day One Publications.

Printed by 4edge Limited

Contents

Acknowledgements **5**

Foreword **6**

Introduction **8**

1 The Apostolic Church **10**

2 The fall of Jerusalem (AD 70) **14**

3 Wider and still wider **18**

4 The empire turns 'Christian' **26**

5 The church in the early Middle Ages **34**

6 The church's response to Islam **42**

7 Medieval dissent **46**

8 First streaks of dawn **52**

9 The darkness deepens but God prepares his way **60**

10 A great light: the sixteenth century Reformation **64**

11 God's Frenchman **73**

12 The English Reformation **80**

Contents

13 Rome's response: the Counter-Reformation **86**

14 Protestant England and her American colonies **90**

15 From 'Christian' republic to constitutional monarchy **98**

16 The First Great Awakening **106**

17 The gospel goes global **114**

18 Revivals and revivalism **120**

19 To the ends of the earth **128**

20 Born in adversity **134**

21 Testing times **138**

22 Redefining the boundaries **145**

23 Evangelical recovery **151**

24 Winds of change **156**

25 The church under Communism **161**

26 New model, new ministries **167**

27 Conclusion **170**

Bibliography **172**

Acknowledgements

I should never have been able to write this book without the help and influence of many people over the course of my life. These include my parents, who introduced me to a Bible-based Christian faith, pastors of churches where I have been in membership, and many others whose impact on my life has contributed to my being able to put pen to paper in this volume.

In particular, thanks are due to Dr Peter Golding, the pastor of Hayes Town Chapel when I was a member there. During the years from 1980 to 1995 he encouraged me to speak from time to time on church history subjects ranging from the apostolic age to the late twentieth century. My notes from those studies have formed the basis for many chapters in this book.

In preparing the manuscript for this book, I am also indebted to Derek French and Andrew Cook, both from Grace Baptist Mission Radio Ministries. Derek in particular has encouraged me throughout and has kindly agreed to write the foreword. Thanks are also due to my wife, Sheila, who has corrected and critiqued the whole manuscript. Comments and encouragements from several members of Mirfield Evangelical Church have also been helpful.

Foreword

A long used cliché concerning the history of the Christian church is that it is 'his story'. In other words, it is the unfolding of God's sovereign plans and purposes to redeem a people for himself through faith in Christ, and therefore behind all that happens is the sovereign overruling and guiding hand of God. The Lord has promised to build his church, and church history helps us to see how he has been and still is doing that great task. It is this fact which makes church history such an important subject for every Christian as we see the way the Lord has been working in our world. It teaches us about the amazing ways of God, which are a constant encouragement to the church in its task of world mission. God has worked powerfully in the past and is well able to do so again. Church history also teaches us important lessons enabling us to grasp the importance of maintaining true biblical doctrine and practice, as well as helping us to avoid the errors and the mistakes of former generations. It helps us to persevere during times of difficulty and persecution, because through church history we learn how God has sustained his people in the hardest of times. This book is an excellent introduction to this most remarkable subject.

It is also fair to say that church history is vast, and many volumes have been written about it, which can be rather daunting for those unfamiliar with the subject. We therefore can be thankful to God that one of the gifts he has given to some of his servants is the ability to summarize huge subjects and condense them into more manageable sizes for us to benefit from. Philip Parsons comes into that category and this book is an excellent example of his work. I have known and worked with Philip on a number of projects over many years, and this particular volume is a welcome addition to other material he has produced. What we have in this book is

Foreword

a panoramic view of the history of the church up to the present day. This needs to be kept in mind while reading it, as quite deliberately he has not been able to include every single detail about the history of the church in a volume of this size, but he has covered its main subjects in a most helpful manner. This should give an appetite to all who read it to consider other writers, and Philip has supplied ample footnotes to help us do this.

Derek French

Introduction

In recent times many books have been published on the subject of church history, and some have covered the whole period from the first coming of Christ into the world up to the present day. So why yet another one? Most of the previously published works on the subject have gone into considerable depth, or have focused mainly on individual characters. Both approaches are excellent and have served their purpose well. For a variety of reasons there are many in our churches who are largely ignorant of church history and who also have difficulty in reading anything of any length. This book is attempting to address this need. In order to achieve this objective I have had to be very selective and have taken a broad-brush approach to the subject. My aim has been to concentrate on major movements and trends, but in an attempt to keep my readers' interest I have tried to include as many brief biographical sketches of the leading players as possible. To the more knowledgeable reader there will be omissions which might be considered vital; but of necessity I have had to choose what to leave out in this epic story which we call the history of the church.

The set of books which was most responsible for first promoting my interest in church history was a Victorian three-volume set by J. A. Wylie with the title, *The History of Protestantism*. I discovered these books in a privately-owned second-hand collection in Bournemouth in the summer of 1967. They cost only a few pounds and were worth every penny I paid for them. Over the course of the next year or so I devoured these tomes (nearly 1900 pages!) and they have undoubtedly shaped my thinking on the subject. They provided me with a framework on which to build any subsequent knowledge I have obtained.

Introduction

But I do not think I would ever have had the interest in the subject which I now do, were it not for one small book I read in the spring of 1967. It was written by Iain Murray and had the title, *The Forgotten Spurgeon*. Our pastor at the time, Patrick Rose, had loaned me the book and I had agreed to read it because of his recommendation. I was in for a big surprise. By the time I had completed the book, I had changed my theological perspective, which in turn revolutionized my whole approach to church history.

Since reading those books, I have also read biographies of many of the leading characters in the history of the church as well as Merle d'Aubigné's *The Reformation in England* and two of the early volumes of Philip Schaff's *History of the Christian Church*.

The sub-title of this book indicates that I have viewed church history from an evangelical perspective. The word evangelical derives from the Greek ευαγγελλιον, meaning 'gospel'. Inasmuch as churches have strayed from being 'gospel' churches, they forfeit the right to being called churches at all and are little more than religious organizations. Over the course of the last 2000 years, sections of the professing church have fallen into this category and I have therefore given them scant coverage in this history.

Even within evangelicalism, many have a parochial view of the church: our church, our denomination, the mission we support. Writing this book has helped me to see the church from a more global perspective, as the great work of God in history, as the kingdom of Christ on earth throughout the whole of the Christian era. It has been a fascinating, illuminating, exciting and encouraging experience. I trust that readers will find it to be the same.

Philip Parsons
(Mirfield)

The Apostolic Church

Beginnings

There is no completely straightforward answer to the question, 'When did Christianity begin?' The answer which a well-informed outsider might give could be that it was obviously begun by Jesus Christ himself when he was here in this world. In one sense the church did begin with the ministry of Christ. And yet that beginning was, on the surface, rather disappointing. Though he was the Son of God, possessing all the attributes of Deity, by the time of his ascension back to heaven the number of true believers was probably less than a thousand (1 Cor. 15:6).

But with the giving of the Holy Spirit on the Day of Pentecost (Acts 2), there was a real change in momentum. Three thousand were converted on that day alone. And what is even more surprising is that these converts were not just local to Jerusalem, but from a wide range of people-groups across the Roman Empire. Luke, the writer of the book of Acts, gives us a summary list of the main nationalities present in Jerusalem on that eventful day. They were 'from every nation under heaven' (Acts 2:5). When examined more closely, Luke's rather 'boring' list of names is very revealing. Some had travelled more than one thousand miles to be in Jerusalem for the festival. The Medes, for instance, came from east of Persia (modern Iran). Others were from Rome, about a thousand miles to the west, while still others came from the southern parts of Egypt, nearly the same distance to the south.

We are talking about people who had travelled to Jerusalem from a huge area—one of the most cosmopolitan congregations to listen to gospel preaching that the world has ever seen. Many had not been born as Jews, but had converted to Judaism; others were very interested in the Jewish religion but had not yet committed themselves to it. The one thing that linked them all was the worship in the temple in Jerusalem on the Day of Pentecost.

They all spoke Greek, the commercial language of the Roman Empire at that time, but as a result of the apostles being given on that occasion the gift of preaching in many foreign languages, these visitors were able to hear the 'wonderful works of God' (Acts 2:11, AV) in their own native tongues. As a result of the apostles' preaching on that day, three thousand received the message and were baptized as Christian believers. So by the end of the day there were believers originating from a large part of the Roman Empire, who would soon carry the gospel back to their fellow countrymen. In the providence and wisdom of God, the New Testament Church had been 'born in a day', with small groups of Christians soon to spread all over the Roman world. The 'apostolic age' of the church had dawned.

The apostles and their ministry

This early period of church history has been referred to as the apostolic age because it was a period clearly dominated by the activities of the apostles and their assistants. This immediately raises the question as to who the apostles were. The Greek word *apostolos* literally means a 'sent one' and it could be used generally in that sense. But to the New Testament writers, the term was also a technical term, used to refer to a specific group of men within the Church (Acts 1:2). They were the twelve men who had been with the Lord throughout his earthly ministry (Acts 1:21–22) and who were witnesses to his resurrection (Acts 1:22). The appointment of Matthias to replace Judas (Acts 1:15–26) confirms this definition of who the apostles were.

What then about the Apostle Paul? How does he fit into this category? There is no doubt that he was an apostle. He was quite clear about the ministry he had been given (Eph. 3:2–8). In his letters he usually addresses

Chapter 1

himself to his readers as an apostle, and in 2 Corinthians chapters 10 to 13 he is at pains to assert and emphasize his apostleship. Even though he was not one of the original twelve, he does meet the criteria required for an apostle. He had seen the risen Christ in person (1 Cor. 15:8) and had been taught the apostolic message by the Lord during his three years in Arabia (Gal. 1:15–18).

During those early days after Pentecost, through the power of the Holy Spirit, the apostles established Christ's church in much of the Roman world. Not only through their preaching, but also through their writings in the New Testament, the Christian message was explained more fully to the early converts. These writings were crucial; without them the Christian church would have disappeared without trace.[1]

The authority of the apostles in the early church was demonstrated by the supervision they exercised over the growing and expanding kingdom of Christ. When the gospel broke new barriers or reached new regions, the apostles were involved in the work or soon came to confirm it. When Philip's evangelistic work in Samaria began to bear fruit, Peter and John were sent down from Jerusalem to confirm it (Acts 8:14–17). The same is true of Peter's visit to the first Gentile convert, Cornelius (Acts 10). Not only did the apostles establish new churches, they appointed officers in those churches: elders (Acts 14:23) and deacons (Acts 6).

Other factors

Clearly, then, the apostles and their preaching played a vital role in establishing the churches throughout the first century Roman world. But they were not the only players. There were other secondary, yet still important factors in the spread of Christianity.

One of these additional factors, surprisingly, was the movement of ordinary Christians. In the first century, the Roman Empire was at its peak and the benefits of the *pax Romana* (Roman peace) could be exploited by those early Christian believers. The well-made roads all across Europe, carrying their frequently high levels of commercial and military traffic, could also be used by individual Roman citizens and others. Then there were significant sea travel facilities. The Apostle Paul and his companions used both modes of travel to maximum effect. Of course, both of these ways of travel could pose dangers. Paul mentions dangers from robbers, presumably in more remote areas, and he was also shipwrecked three times (2 Cor. 11:25).

But others, too, were able to travel freely. Lydia, the first convert in Europe, had settled in Philippi, several hundred miles distant from her native Thyatira. Even the runaway slave, Onesimus (Philemon 10), had been able to make his way from Colosse to Rome (more than five hundred miles). As the church began to grow, the relocation of believers across the empire meant that, in effect, small churches sprang up over a wide area.

It is thus a sheer fact of history that from a handful of disciples the church of Jesus Christ multiplied and grew, not only during the days of the apostles but for the next two hundred years. It has been estimated that by the accession of Constantine as emperor in AD 306, the number of Christians was about 10% of the Empire.[2] Some historians put this at five million Christians.

NOTES

1 'The apostolic gospel ... as preserved for us in the New Testament, is still the foundation of the Church.' J. Gresham Machen, *The New Testament, an Introduction to its Literature and History*, (Edinburgh: Banner of Truth Trust, 1990), p. 15.

2 Generally accepted estimate: e.g. Philip Schaff, *History of the Christian Church*, vol. 2, p. 19.

The fall of Jerusalem (AD 70)

When the gospel was first preached to the Jews in Jerusalem on the Day of Pentecost, three thousand believed. In those early days of the church, Jerusalem was the centre from which gospel light radiated far and wide. And by AD 50, due to the missionary efforts of the apostles, particularly Paul and his companions, the gospel had spread to Egypt, Syria and much of Southern Europe, including Rome.

As the church expanded, with individual churches being established in many different places across Europe and the Middle East, Jerusalem was no longer at the centre of things. From the very beginning, many Jewish people had been hostile to the newly-formed Christian church, and by the time Paul was arrested in Jerusalem around AD 58 (Acts 21), the hostility of the Jews had hardened. There is no record of even the church in Jerusalem helping him or coming to his defence at that time! At the time of Paul's arrest, the Roman Procurator of Judea was Festus (Acts 25:1–12), who died just three years later in AD 61.

In the three-month gap between the death of Festus and the arrival of his replacement, the Jews wasted no time. James, one of the leaders of the Jerusalem Church (probably the writer of the New Testament letter which bears his name), along with some other Christians, were arrested by the High Priest. These believers were then, in the absence of the Roman authorities, tried by the Jews and stoned to death. What a devastating blow this must have been to the Jewish Christians in Jerusalem! It must have made them wonder whether it was worth continuing to belong to this despised sect and many were doubtless tempted to revert to Judaism.

It was about this time that the letter to the Hebrews was written to speak to just such a situation. In that letter, the writer demonstrates that the new covenant in Christ has now superseded the old. Many warnings

The fall of Jerusalem (AD 70)

are given against Jewish believers turning back from their position of greater privilege as Christians to the old order of things. Hebrews also has a reference to the cessation of the sacrificial system associated with the temple worship (Heb. 10:8–10), and Jesus himself had predicted that the temple would be destroyed (Matt. 24:2).

As the tension in Israel was beginning to rise, the letter to the Hebrews was a timely warning. A succession of evil and incompetent Roman procurators, coupled with mounting resentment among the Jews, meant that war was not far off. All this came to a head when the Jews seized control of the city and annihilated the Roman garrison. By this time, Jewish extremists had gained control of the south-east of the country as well as Galilee and Transjordan. Of course, all this was completely unacceptable to the Roman authorities. The Twelfth Legion was ordered to march south from Syria and attempted to storm the now fortified temple area. But they were repulsed and many were killed as they retreated. The Jews were cock-a-hoop and considered this an omen of future success.

It seems that at this point the Christians then living in Jerusalem took the opportunity of a lull in the fighting to make their escape from the city. It is not completely certain, but is likely that they settled in a place called Pella, situated to the east of the River Jordan. They had heeded the warning given by Jesus in Luke 21:21–22.

In the meantime, the veteran Roman soldier, Vespasian, was given the task of subduing the Jewish revolt in Palestine. In AD 67 he marched through Galilee and quelled the rebellion there, and along the way acquired an unusual friend, the Jewish historian Josephus. Most of the main Galilean towns were sacked in this campaign. Some of the bolder Jews from Galilee made their way up to Jerusalem. By the early summer of AD 68, Vespasian and his army were approaching Jerusalem, when they received news of the death of the Emperor Nero. Civil war in Rome followed, and the Jews in Jerusalem were further buoyed up, thinking that the empire was beginning to crumble.

Chapter 2

In July 69, Vespasian was proclaimed emperor and returned to Rome to restore stability to the Empire. His son, Titus, took control of the conquest of Judea and by the spring of 70 began to besiege Jerusalem. It is an amazing fact that just before the Roman army began to surround the city, a vast number of Jews flocked to it for the Passover, confident that no harm would befall them. They could not have been more wrong, as in the final stages of the siege, the vast majority perished either from famine or the sword. Those taken prisoner were either sold as slaves or were kept for the Roman games, to be thrown to the lions in the arena.

By May 70, half of the city was in the hands of the Romans. Titus then offered the Jewish defenders terms for surrender, which they contemptuously rejected. On 17 July the daily sacrifice in the temple ceased. Step by step the Romans advanced until by 8 August the temple went up in flames. The majority in the city at that time did not survive. Josephus estimates that during the siege over a million died and about one hundred thousand were taken prisoner. During the fire, the vast amount of gold adorning the temple building had melted and run down between the huge stones. In order to extract the gold, the temple was then completely demolished (stone by stone) except the foundation abutment supporting the west wall (this is now called the Wailing Wall). The rest of the city was also rendered uninhabitable. The treasures taken from the city made the Roman soldiers so rich that the value of gold in that part of the world dropped dramatically.

Thus was the terrible end of Jerusalem and in particular of the temple, fulfilling precisely the words of Christ in Luke 21:6. But what was its significance in the history of the Church? Two points are of particular note:

Firstly, as an act of Divine providence it marked a decisive end to Old Testament religion. If the Jews as a nation had received Jesus as their Messiah, then they would have brought the Old Testament system of sacrifices to a conclusion themselves. But because most of them rejected the Christian message, God had to step in in judgement to destroy the temple.

The fall of Jerusalem (AD 70)

Secondly, although not a single inhabitant was left in Jerusalem on that fateful day and it seemed as if the nation of Israel would disappear, God has against all the odds wonderfully preserved the Jews as a nation and permitted them to return to their homeland in 1948. Are they yet to play a vital role in the final chapter of the church's history?

Wider and still wider

Apart from the relatively small number of Christians living in the land of Israel, the Jewish war which ended with the fall of Jerusalem had only a minimal effect on the church as a whole.

By AD 70, Asia Minor (modern-day Turkey) and Greece had become the cradle of expanding Christianity. The apostles had established the church so thoroughly in those parts, that by around the year AD 100 the pagan temples were almost forsaken. In the second century, Christianity penetrated eastwards into Mesopotamia and Armenia. In the south, churches were soon established in Egypt, with Alexandria becoming one of the most influential centres of Christianity of that time. The church also spread into North Africa and westwards into most of southern Europe, including Italy, Spain and Gaul (France). Even in those early days there is evidence that the gospel had also reached some parts of Britain.

During this period of expansion, the church influenced and affected all classes and social groups. It was not restricted to one class only, but rich and poor, high and low were to be found within its ranks. While the poorer classes were more numerous in the churches, demonstrating the redeeming and comforting power of the gospel, others from the educated and higher classes were also attracted to the new religion. During the persecution by the Emperor Domitian in the 90s, among the victims were one of his relatives, Flavia Domitian, and her husband, Flavius Clemens. Even the Roman writer Pliny bemoans the fact that 'men of every rank go over to Christianity'. In terms of learning and scholarship, early church leaders like Justin Martyr, Irenaeus, Clement, Tertullian and Cyprian excelled or at least equalled their pagan contemporaries in talent and learning.

Against the tide

Yes, the church grew; yes, it attracted 'all sorts and conditions of men'; but remarkably, this expansion and growth took place in the most unfavourable of circumstances. At first the church was ignored by the Romans as being merely a Jewish sect. Then it was slandered, proscribed and persecuted. At times the punishments for just being a Christian were confiscation of property or even death. The demands of the gospel for repentance, faith, and renunciation of self and the world made Christianity unpopular with many. Some would have preferred to earn their salvation or wished to cling onto their worldly pleasures.

The Jewish origin of the church also offended the pride of the Greeks and Romans, as did the poverty of many of its adherents (very far removed from the 'prosperity gospel' of recent times!). Yet despite this unfavourable climate, the church planted by the apostles continued to grow until it had spread over most of the Roman world.

From a human point of view, to what can we attribute this steady yet sustained growth of the church? If, despite many obstacles, it grew from a few hundred when Christ ascended into heaven to an estimated five million by the early fourth century, what were the reasons for this remarkable expansion?

One misconceived notion as to the 'success' of the early church is that Christians continued to work the kind of miracles which Christ and his apostles had been able to work. But this does not fit the facts. The 'signs of the apostles', a designation which the Apostle Paul gives the miracles (2 Cor. 12:12), died away with the apostolic age. A few tried to hang on to them, but the reported incidents of miracles in the second and third centuries is extremely low and only increases during the fourth and fifth centuries. Many of these later 'miracles' were associated with the tombs of the martyrs and bear little resemblance to those recorded in the New Testament.

Chapter 3

One cause of the success of the Christian gospel was (and still is) its own intrinsic moral and spiritual value when compared with any other philosophy or religion. No other religion claims divinity for its human founder. There is no belief so simple yet profound as salvation through the death of a perfect substitute. There is no moral ethic as elevated as the Sermon on the Mount. There is no other teaching capable of producing the degree of godly living in its followers that genuine Christianity does. No philosophy of those times had such an emancipating effect on women and the home life over which they presided. No other faith ever showed such concern for the poor and suffering, and gave its confessors such assurance in the face of death.

Another factor which aided the advance of the gospel in those early days was the corrupt and decaying condition of the pagan world into which the gospel was first preached. With the fall of Jerusalem in AD 70, the surviving Jews had been scattered all over the empire, and Judaism had no real national existence or influence. The early energy of Greek science and art was much diminished and the moral tone of earlier Roman emperors was a thing of the past. In such a climate, the new religion commended itself to those who were prepared to think, as the only hope in the increasing moral gloom. In the fourth century, Augustine writes that 'Christ appeared, to the men of a decrepit and decaying world, as one who could give new life.'

In spite of persecution

The very first persecution of the church was by the Jews. Severe though this may have seemed, it was eclipsed by the persecution under the Roman emperors. To those who have some appreciation of the nature of the Roman Empire, it might in certain respects come as a surprise that the church was persecuted at all. The policy of imperial Rome was in general tolerant, and freedom of thought was allowed. The state did not control education but left it to the individual. The religions of the conquered races were tolerated as long as they did not interfere with the interests of the state. Even the Jews had enjoyed special protection since the time of Julius Caesar. At the beginning, with the Christian church being considered as a Jewish sect, under the providence of God Christianity became established in the leading cities of the empire before its true character was understood (Acts 18:12–17).

But as soon as Christianity was understood as a religion claiming universal acceptance and validity, it was branded as unlawful and treasonable. 'You have no right to exist' then became the oft-repeated cry. What then were the main reasons for the empire seeking to destroy the church?

In the first place the Roman state was thoroughly interwoven with pagan idolatry. The success of the legions was attributed to the gods. The priests and Vestal Virgins were supported out of the public treasury and the emperor was considered unofficially as 'Pontifex Maximus' (Chief Priest) and regarded as an object of worship. Clearly, the Christian teaching came into collision with these ideals. Rome also saw the Christian faith as a rival because it was a universal religion, not merely a national faith.

Then again, many activities of the Christians aroused the suspicion of conspiracy against the state. Christians became known for their refusal to worship the emperor or join in idolatrous ceremonies at public functions. Some showed a reluctance to take part in military service and disregarded involvement in politics. It soon became clear that the Christians were motivated by spiritual and eternal issues rather than temporal ones. All these factors drew down upon the church the suspicion of hostility to the Caesars and the Roman people.

A further factor was the generally superstitious nature of the common people. Rumours of incest and cannibalism were readily entertained because of the nature of some Christian ceremonies, e.g. the Lord's Supper. These superstitious ideas soon led to the Christians becoming the scapegoats for all kinds of calamities.

Chapter 3

Because the church was persecuted for nearly two hundred and fifty years during Roman times, two questions obviously arise. Was this persecution all over the empire and was it continuous? The answer to both is in the negative. The persecutions were often very localized and came in approximately ten waves, with quite long periods of respite between them. Often the attitude of the emperor was the determining factor. Some of the best emperors in terms of their ability to rule were the most violent of persecutors, while others left the church alone, out of sheer indifference and their absorption with partying and promiscuity.

The severity, too, of these persecutions was quite variable. Sometimes confiscation of property and exile were the main instruments used. At other times Christians were crucified, thrown to wild animals in the arena, executed by the sword, slowly burned in boiling pitch or just left to die in a dungeon. Although ordinary Christians were not exempt, often church leaders were the victims. Ignatius (circa 107), Polycarp (155), Justin Martyr (166) and Cyprian (258) were among the church leaders who fell during successive persecutions.

The Christians' Last Prayer, by Jean-Léon Gérôme

Wider and still wider

There is a further important question: How did the church react to persecution?

Although the response of Christians to persecution varied, by and large the spirit with which those early Christians bore their sufferings shines out as one of the proofs of the genuineness of the Christian faith. But sadly, not all stood firm during the storm. Those who did stand and were put to death were called 'martyrs'. Those who stood but were not called upon to make that ultimate sacrifice were called 'confessors'. But there were also some who denied their faith and the Lord they had once confessed: these were dubbed the 'lapsed'.

But just as there were weak ones who apostatized, there were also fanatics who embraced martyrdom with a misguided zeal. Generally speaking, church leaders counselled otherwise. Clement of Alexandria said, 'The Lord himself has commanded us to flee to another city if we are persecuted.'

Despite the fanatical zeal of some and the weakness and apostasy of others, the martyrdoms of the first three centuries of the church remain one of the noblest spectacles of history and an evidence of the indestructible nature of authentic Christianity.

We do need to add this cautionary note, that perhaps one of the church's abuses of martyrdom was the way the martyrs became venerated as higher-grade Christians, with the anniversaries of their deaths being celebrated. Visits to their tombs were sometimes claimed to be accompanied by miracles. It is undoubtedly true that this misguided attitude towards the martyrs laid the foundation for the veneration of 'saints' which grew up in the Middle Ages.

Propagation

If the early Christian church grew in this quite remarkable way against all the odds, what methods of propagating the gospel were used? We with our twenty-first century mind-set would possibly have expected to find that there were evangelistic campaigns, large missionary organizations and a

Chapter 3

host of full-time Christian workers in evangelism. When we look at the facts, we find exactly the opposite.

After the days of the apostles, no names of great missionaries are mentioned until the beginning of the Middle Ages. There were no missionary societies or organized efforts in evangelism during the whole of the three hundred years from the death of the Apostle John. And yet by the end of the fourth century, the whole of the Roman world was nominally 'Christianized'.

If there were no special means or agencies for the propagation of the gospel, can we discover why it flourished in those early days? The evidence points to three main ingredients.

(a) Bible-based preaching

Following the apostles' example, the early church continued to preach the message of salvation through repentance towards God and faith in Christ. Although forced to meet in houses or sometimes in secret, preaching continued to dominate church life. It had not been displaced either by the sacraments, as happened in the Middle Ages, or by music, singing and drama, as in modern times. And it was largely preaching in the context of the worshipping community.

(b) Consistent Christian living

The early Christians took the many New Testament exhortations to holy living very seriously. In those early days, being a Christian was a costly business, and few hypocrites ventured into the Christian community. Whatever their rank or position, these wholehearted believers 'gossiped' the gospel to others around them. 'The Christian told his neighbour—the labourer [told] his fellow-labourer, the slave his fellow-slave, the servant his master or mistress—the message of salvation.'[1] Where this verbal witness was backed up by consistent Christian living, then it became, as it still is today, one of the most effective means of evangelism.

(c) Bible translation

Although in the first century Greek as the language of commerce provided an excellent vehicle for conveying the Christian message, it soon became necessary for the Bible to be translated into various other languages. The New Testament writings had been completed with the publication of the Apostle John's Revelation and letters. These documents were circulated among the churches and it was not long before the complete canon of Scripture had become generally accepted. Early manuscript evidence shows that even the order of the New Testament books had been established by the early third century. Early translations of the Bible were made into Latin, Syriac and Egyptian.

**

It was through these three simple methods that God planted his church in those early days: Bible-based preaching, personal witness backed up by consistent Christian living, and Bible translation. Probably the area in which we in the church today fall down most is that of consistent Christian living. Lindsay Brown, speaking at the Evangelical Movement of Wales' Conference in Aberystwyth in 2014, said that 'the greatest hindrance to the growth of the church today is the inconsistency of the lives of professing Christians'.

NOTE

1 Philip Schaff, *History of the Christian Church*, vol. 2, p. 18.

The empire turns 'Christian'

The most significant figure who steps onto the stage of church history at the beginning of the fourth century is the first 'Christian' emperor, Constantine the Great. He became emperor at the relatively young age of 34, in the place of his father, who died in York in 306.

Although he seems always to have been favourably disposed towards Christianity, his public commitment to the faith took place in October 312 at the Battle of Milvian Bridge near Rome. Just prior to the battle, he claimed that he saw a shining cross in the sky and declared, 'By this sign I conquer.' He had the sign of the cross put on his battle standard and cited this as the reason for his victory. It has been much disputed as to what kind of Christian Constantine really was. It may well be that he saw that the Christians were becoming so numerous that his conversion was more a matter of convenience than conviction.

For better or for worse, the conversion of Emperor Constantine marks one of the most significant turning points in the history of Christianity. Some of the changes which

The bronze statue of Constantine in York

26 A Beginner's Guide to Church History

The empire turns 'Christian'

came about following his conversion set the scene in the church for many centuries to come, and in some respects right up to the present day.

Positively, the accession of Constantine resulted in a number of benefits for the church:

The victory of Christianity over paganism

Despite persecution by a succession of pagan emperors, the despised sect of the Christians had kept on growing and growing until it had reached around 10% of the empire—a sizeable minority. With Constantine in power, not only did the persecution cease, but Christians were actively encouraged, confiscated property was restored, and there was a long period of peace and calm for the churches. To be a Christian not only became tolerated, but now almost fashionable. In the almost three hundred years since Pentecost, the severest testing for the church had been the fires of persecution. She had largely come through this 'fiery trial' with flying colours.

Clearer definition of major doctrines

Even before the early fourth century, the Biblical doctrines concerning the nature of God, the deity of Christ and the deity of the Holy Spirit had been challenged. Some of the New Testament letters are written with certain Gnostic[1] heresies in mind. But in the years following Constantine's accession, two major controversies are particularly worthy of note. The first of these was the Arian controversy, named after its chief proponent, Arius, a presbyter in one of the churches in Egypt. Arian theology strongly resembles modern-day Jehovah's Witness teachings concerning the doctrine of the Trinity. Because the church became deeply divided by the controversy, in 325 the Emperor Constantine called for a council at Nicaea in north-western Turkey. After considerable debate, the council produced the Nicene Creed, its content being very much influenced by a young deacon, Athanasius. But this was not the end of the matter, as

Chapter 4

Arius and his supporters launched a campaign to discredit Athanasius. For forty years he was criticized, deposed, exiled and hunted around the East and Europe. At times he felt so alone in his defence of the truth, that the phrase *Athanasius contra mundum* ('Athanasius against the world') was coined. Eventually Athanasius' Biblically-based views were accepted by the church at the Council of Constantinople in 381, eight years after he had died. The whole controversy produced the magnificent Nicene Creed and later the Athanasian Creed, both of which are excellent statements of the doctrines of the Trinity and the full deity of Christ.

Later in the fourth century and early fifth century, other important doctrines were debated and better defined. One such concerned sin and grace—the Pelagian controversy, named after the British monk who precipitated it. Pelagius was an earnest preacher who was shocked by the low state of moral behaviour in the church, particularly in the churches in Rome. The doctrine in his preaching was based upon the assumption that man is basically good, and free to live a good life, if only he will make the effort. Pelagius denied the teaching of Paul in Romans 5, that all of humanity is born in a state of sin, because of Adam's fall (Gen. 3). In the ensuing controversy with Pelagius, Augustine became famous in his defence of the truth. Two statements by him encapsulate the essence of his position: 'In Adam's fall, we sinned all,' and 'Give what you command and then command what you will.' The big emphasis in Augustine's statements is on the free unmerited grace of God, over against man's free will. Although not all followed Augustine's views, the church owes a great debt to this great theologian of grace.

A number of notable Christian leaders arose during these years

This was the age of the 'Church Fathers' (not to be confused with earlier leaders who followed the apostles and were called the 'Apostolic Fathers').

We have already mentioned Athanasius and Augustine. Other outstanding leaders were John Chrysostom, a gifted preacher in Antioch, and Ambrose of Milan, under whose preaching Augustine was converted. It has been observed that, in the clarity of their teaching, these 'Church Fathers' seem to overshadow all the 'Apostolic Fathers' of the second and third centuries.

The publication of a Latin Bible

When the New Testament was written, it was written in Greek, which was then the language of the Roman Empire. With the passage of time, as Latin began to replace Greek as the *lingua franca* in the western part of the empire, it was important for the Scriptures to be available in Latin. There were also variants of Latin spoken in different regions. In the late fourth century, a reclusive scholar, Jerome, undertook the translation of the whole Bible into Latin. Jerome's translation (now called the Vulgate) had the effect of standardising the Latin used across the whole of the empire. He had provided a common version for all to read.

Unfortunately, Jerome's Latin Bible was a mixed blessing for the church. This was because it had within it a distorted understanding of the gospel.[2] It was Jerome's distortion of the gospel which contributed to some of the fundamental errors of both Roman Catholicism and Eastern Orthodoxy.

***

But despite these positive features, the post-Constantine era was to constitute a much more subtle time of testing for the people of God. Some of the negative effects following Constantine's accession were:

The church drifted into further error

We have already seen that during the peaceful period for the church brought in by Constantine, a number of important doctrines were debated and better defined. But there were also other errors which had begun to be accepted in an embryonic form during the second and third centuries, which now began to be more fully developed.

Chapter 4

(A) BAPTISMAL ERRORS

So much value was placed upon baptism in the early centuries, that for converts to the faith in the third and fourth centuries, baptism was often delayed until just before death. The necessity of baptism to salvation was also taught by the end of the fourth century. It can be easily seen that these ideas naturally fed into the doctrine of baptismal regeneration,[3] which became commonly held throughout medieval times.

(B) THE LORD'S SUPPER

During the first three centuries, there was no adoration of the 'host', no altar, no 'sacrifice' in the communion service. But the elements used in communion services increasingly began to be regarded as having an inherent sanctity after consecration. The full doctrine of transubstantiation,[4] however, was not accepted until the ninth century.

(C) PAGAN IDOLATRY WITH A 'CHRISTIAN' VENEER

With the changed attitude of the state towards Christianity, many 'religious' pagans professed conversion and consequently brought their pagan ideas into the church. For example, the use of images and pictures in Christian worship only began after Constantine. As William Cunningham puts it, 'All the leading features of paganism, under a Christian form',[5] were now introduced into Christian worship.

Alliance between church and state

In the post-Constantine era of the Roman Empire, there was a gradual change in the relationship between church and state. Up until that time, the state had either been hostile or indifferent towards the church. Now, with the emperor himself a professing Christian, everything began to change. Church leaders gave the emperor a position of prominence in the church because of his civil status. Constantine presided at the Council of Nicaea in 325. Understandable though this was, it was not in line with the teaching of the New Testament, where leadership was to be on the basis of spiritual qualities, not just administrative ability or political status.

As the church moved into the Middle Ages, the unbiblical notion of the 'Christian state' became almost universally accepted. Even at the Reformation, the Reformers, to a man, were unable to see that this concept had no foundation in the New Testament. Because of this error, the Reformers were sometimes guilty of conniving with the civil authorities in the persecution of their opponents. The idea of a 'Christian country' still persists in some European countries today.

Church government

During apostolic days, the churches were governed by a plurality of elders, supported by deacons. As churches became larger, the 'president' among the elders became known as a bishop. By the early fourth century, the separate, superior office of bishop was widely recognized. In large cities there were often many congregations, and the bishop eventually became the head of the churches in that region. Thus, by default, the beginnings of a hierarchy were emerging, generally unchallenged by the people, but nowhere found in the New Testament.

Up until this time, unsuccessful attempts had also been made by the bishops of Rome to gain the ascendancy. But now with the Roman emperor supporting the church, the concept of Roman supremacy began to develop in the church. When the Western Empire fell in 476, the bishops of Rome effectively filled the vacuum and became the 'heirs' of the Roman imperial succession. With the progress of time, the power of the papacy increased. Not all heads of state welcomed this development, and disputes between popes and monarchs rumbled on throughout the medieval period. As we shall see in later chapters, Britain in particular often showed an independent spirit, culminating eventually in Henry VIII's break with Rome.

Chapter 4

The rise of monasticism[6]

As we have already noted, during the first three hundred years of the church's life an attitude had grown up which regarded the martyrs as a superior 'class' of Christians. They were viewed as the spiritual elite, and their tombs were places where they were given excessive veneration. Now that the church was experiencing peace and rest from outward persecution, the spiritual 'elite' role was expanded to include a growing number of monks and hermits. During the times of persecution, the church had been a society largely separate from the world. Now, with no antagonistic state inflicting punishments which helped to maintain the purity of the church, monastic orders sprang up. These orders devised their own masochistic rituals as an aid to personal holiness. The 'pillar saints' were a feature of this period, where 'holy' men would live on the top of a pillar. The higher the pillar, the holier the man! Even great leaders like Augustine were carried away with the notion that monasticism was 'the surest and shortest way to heaven'. The Augustinian monastic order was later named after him.

***

The question naturally arises, 'Why did the church accept and adopt such clearly non-Biblical teachings and practices?' The following are possible reasons:

(a) Although the Nicene Creed shows a solid grasp of Scripture, the church did not seem to be clear on the principle of 'Sola Scriptura'. The Reformers understood this principle to mean that the Bible should be the church's only rule of faith and practice. Tradition, although it could be helpful, should always be subservient to Scripture.

(b) The emerging hierarchical model of church government prevailed over the simpler biblical pattern, probably for pragmatic reasons.

(c) Because the idea of baptismal regeneration was becoming increasingly accepted, the biblical teaching on the new birth (John 3:3–8) seems to have been inadequately understood. During the Middle Ages, mere mental assent to basic Christian doctrine was regarded as sufficient for anyone to be regarded as a Christian.

Another lesson we can learn from this period of church history is that outward peace for the church is often a mixed blessing. It can lead to real progress, but it also can have within it the seeds of spiritual decline. By and large, the church is a plant which grows best in winter!

NOTES

1. Gnosticism was a prominent heretical movement of the second-century Christian church, partly of pre-Christian origin. Among other things, Gnostic teachings were usually opposed to the Biblical truths of the real humanity of Christ and his bodily resurrection. Jehovah's Witnesses have imbibed some Gnostic views.
2. Jerome's translation of key New Testament passages was a serious distortion of essential truth. Two areas of false teaching which have come from the Vulgate Bible are (a) the translation of the Greek word for 'repentance', which literally means 'change mind', as 'do penance'; and (b) the translation of the once-for-all sacrifice of Christ referred to in Hebrews 10:12 with a tense implying the continual offering of his sacrifice. The power of the Roman Catholic priesthood has been built upon Jerome's incorrect translation of this verse.
3. Baptismal regeneration is the belief that when a person in baptized in the name of the Trinity, they are thereby born again of the Holy Spirit, and that marks the beginning of their life as a Christian.
4. Transubstantiation is the belief that when the priest utters the words of consecration of the elements in the communion service, the elements are changed into the body and blood of Christ. This belief was not fully endorsed by the pope until the twelfth century.
5. William Cunningham, *Historical Theology*, vol. 1 (London: Banner of Truth Trust, 1960), p. 201.
6. Monasticism is a religious way of life in which one is celibate and renounces worldly pursuits to devote oneself fully to spiritual activities, often in a community. Monastic life plays an important role in the Roman Catholic and Orthodox traditions, but has no foundation in the New Testament.

The church in the early Middle Ages

The period of time known as the Middle Ages stretches approximately from the fall of Rome in 476 through to the Reformation, a period of around one thousand years. Even though, politically, the end of the Roman Empire was a seismic event, because the church at that time was a monolithic organization, 476 came and went with relatively little impact upon church life. Indeed, it would be true to say that the church, as a large, cohesive organization, provided stability in an otherwise decaying and collapsing world. Certainly, Leo, the bishop of Rome during those turbulent years, made a significant contribution in negotiating with the barbarians who were threatening the city. Leo I, as he later became known, is reckoned by many as being the first pope. His activities at that time strengthened his claim to 'supremacy' over the church.

East and West

When Constantine came to power, he decided to establish his seat of power in Byzantium on the north side of the Bosphorus. He completely rebuilt the city and renamed it Constantinople (modern Istanbul). He appointed a deputy in Rome to oversee the affairs of the western part of the Empire. When the city of Rome fell to the Barbarians in 476, the western part of the Empire fragmented. The eastern part, however, continued with Constantinople as its capital and Greek as its language. Although there was not an official split in the church at that time, inevitably the eastern and western churches drifted further apart in both doctrine and practice.

The church in the early Middle Ages

With the fragmentation of the Western Empire, the Latin language which had been its *lingua franca* gradually fell into disuse. The various nation states reverted to using their native languages and dialects. This meant that it was not long before the Bible became a closed book to the majority. Only those educated enough to learn Latin would have been able to read it. Without the Bible in the language of the people, and a literate populace, the gospel became largely obscured. During the Middle Ages, a properly-informed understanding of the Christian gospel was gradually replaced by assent to a minimal Christian formula, plus adherence to rituals and ceremonies of various kinds.

Alongside this loss of the Bible, the power of the church hierarchy was increasing. Those among the priests, bishops and cardinals who were corrupt soon realized that it was in their interest to keep the laity in ignorance. It meant that the church could define both doctrine and practice without being challenged by the common people.

Light in the north of Britain

Throughout the long history of God's people, it has often been true that when gospel light fades in one place, it shines out more brightly elsewhere. This was certainly true of the early Middle Ages. When gospel light was waning in much of mainland Europe, it burned more brightly in the north of Britain.

As we saw in chapter 2, during the first three hundred years of the church's history, for a variety of reasons, churches were planted throughout the Roman Empire. During the second century, there was considerable trade between Europe and the British Isles, and it is likely that some of the merchants who came to English shores were also Christians. Then there were those taken prisoner of war during the Roman expansion in Britain, who were sent back to Rome to work (often as galley slaves). They may well have come into contact with Christians during their time away from home. We also know that there were Christians in the Roman legions, and

Chapter 5

these too could have influenced the beginnings of the church in Britain. However it happened, we are certain that the gospel did come to Britain in those early years, for, when writing about AD 200, Tertullian makes the following remarkable statement: 'Parts of Britain were inaccessible to the Romans but have yielded to Christ.'

Patrick's mission to Ireland

In 373, Calpurnius, one of the deacons of the church in Dumbarton (western Scotland), had a son born to him whom he named Sucat (meaning 'warlike'). The boy soon showed signs of leadership, but no interest in the gospel. When he was in his mid teens, he was playing on the beach with his two sisters when some Irish pirates kidnapped all three of them and sold them in Antrim, Northern Ireland. Sucat was sent into the fields to feed pigs. It was while alone in this situation that something of what he had been taught as a child came back to him (probably the parable of the prodigal son). He came under conviction of sin and turned to Christ in repentance. He poured out his prayers in the solitude of the woods and fields of this foreign land. Sucat eventually returned to his home in Scotland, but felt a strong desire to return to Ireland to preach the gospel to the pagans of the land of his captivity. He changed his name to Patrick and returned to Ulster. His preaching was accompanied with considerable success. Many believed, and a strong church was planted there. Patrick died at the age of 90 in 463.

While the Irish were receiving the gospel, English Christianity came under attack. This time it was from the invading Saxons. In 449, Hengist and Horsa began their conquest of Britain. Christianity was driven back into the western fringes: Wales, Cumbria and Cornwall. Thus much of England became enveloped in the thick darkness of Saxon paganism, with temples of Thor being erected where Christian churches had been before.

About one hundred years after the death of Patrick, a man from Donegal, by the name of Columba, set sail in a coracle from Ireland for

Scotland. 'I will go', he said, 'and preach the word of God in Scotland.' He and his fellow missionaries landed in the Hebrides and set up a chapel on the barren and rocky island of Iona. Though Columba and his fellow missionaries did not have the fuller light of Reformation times, gospel light still burned brightly in Iona at that time. Today, Iona is mainly remembered for its monastery, but in those early days it was more of a School of Theology and a Missionary Training College. Columba and his colleagues initially lived in wooden huts and built a wooden church.

The theological position of those early Christians on Iona is best summed up in their own words:
- The Holy Scriptures are the only rule of faith.
- Throw aside all merit of works, and look for salvation to the grace of God alone.
- Beware of a religion which consists of outward observances. It is better to keep your heart pure before God than to abstain from meats.
- One alone is your head, Jesus Christ.
- Bishops and presbyters are equal; they should be the husbands of one wife, and have their children in subjection.[1]

The missionary zeal of Columba and his colleagues soon spread, and they established other centres in Bangor (County Down), and later in North Wales. From Iona and Bangor, missionaries were sent out to evangelize Europe.

The first missionary venture into Europe was headed by a younger contemporary of Columba, called Columbanus. In the early seventh century, he and twelve companions set sail for Burgundy (eastern France). At first their preaching was well received, and a significant number burned their wooden idols and believed the Christian message. After some years, they encountered opposition both from the Roman Catholic clergy and local rulers. The main reason for this opposition was Columbanus' outspoken criticism of professing Christians who lived inconsistent lives. Columbanus was imprisoned, and when eventually

Chapter 5

released, he and his fellow-workers were expelled from Burgundy. They decided to travel south-east to Zurich in Switzerland. Here again, their message was well received and many professed faith. Columbanus expected to stay for the rest of his days in Switzerland, but by now the Burgundian jurisdiction had spread to Switzerland, and Columbanus and his men had to leave. The Irish evangelists, now well advanced in years, trekked through the rugged mountain terrain to Lombardy (north Italy). Many did not survive the journey, but Columbanus and a handful of his comrades were able to preach the gospel to the pagan Lombards. A monastery in Bobbio, Lombardy, is testimony to this seventh-century Irish mission to Europe.

In those days, the missionaries from Iona were more successful than the Church of Rome in spreading the Christian faith. There was, however, a significant weakness in their strategy: they made no serious attempt to evangelize the Saxon invaders in England. They found that their victors were disinclined to listen to those whom they had conquered. In leaving England largely unevangelized, the Celtic church left the field wide open for missionaries from Rome. In 597, the Pope authorized Augustine (not the fourth-century church leader) to come with a group of forty Benedictine monks to 'convert' the English. In the long term this sounded the death-knell for Iona and Bangor; by the end of the seventh century their distinctively Bible-based Christianity was eventually displaced by the 'Roman Catholic' version.

But even though the 'Roman Catholic' version of Christianity dominated Britain from that time, the preaching of Patrick in Ireland, followed by the missionary endeavours of Columba and his successors, left an indelible mark on these islands and beyond. Although seemingly buried for centuries, the evangelicalism of the primitive church in Britain laid the foundation for a continuing struggle with Rome, which came to full fruition in the Protestant Reformation of the sixteenth century.

The church in the early Middle Ages

The rise of Islam

The religion generally referred to as Islam originated in the seventh century, when Mohammed claimed to have been given special revelations from God. He received most of these 'revelations' in the year 611 while alone in a cave, and he claimed that they were mediated through the angel Gabriel.

The main teachings of Islam (sometimes known as the 5 pillars) are:
(a) The confession that there is one God and that Mohammed is his prophet.
(b) Prayer, five times a day, facing Mecca.
(c) Giving of alms.
(d) Fasting during the month of Ramadan.
(e) Pilgrimage to Mecca at least once during one's lifetime.

In the Koran, Mohammed recognized some of the prophets in the Bible, but he recast them in a new mould. For instance, he referred to Moses the lawgiver as the prophet to show God's clemency and providence. King Solomon he deemed to be the prophet showing God's wisdom, majesty and glory, and Jesus he designated as the prophet showing God's righteousness, omniscience and power. These designations of Biblical characters only partially reflect how Scripture views them. Above all else, Christ is revealed in Scripture, not just as one among many prophets, but as the eternal Son of God, utterly unique.

Although Mohammed's new teaching was initially opposed by many of his contemporaries, it was not long before support for Islam began to grow, until it had become a force to be reckoned with. In line with the concept of Mohammed being the 'prophet of the sword', Islamic forces swept through North Africa, Syria, Persia, and much of the rest of the Middle East. Thousands of Christian churches were either destroyed or converted into mosques. By the early eighth century, Christianity had all but disappeared in these areas. Muslim forces advanced as far as Constantinople (modern Istanbul), but were unable to overthrow it.

Chapter 5

After a protracted period of fighting, in 679 the Muslim Caliph and the Byzantine Emperor Constantine IV agreed on a cessation of hostilities. While the Muslim advance was halted at the south-east border of Europe, in 711 the Arab armies crossed the Straits of Gibraltar and entered Spain. Within a few years, they had crossed the Pyrenees into France, but in 732 they were defeated by the Franks[2] under the leadership of Charles Martel (the Hammer). The Muslims then retreated into Spain, where they remained dominant for over 700 years.

Reviewing these events, some subsequent Christian historians have regarded this Islamic expansion as a divine chastisement on the churches in those countries, largely because of their departure from the truth and increasing idolatry in their worship. The Lord had removed the 'lampstand' from those regions (Rev. 2:5). It is interesting to contrast the effect that opposition and persecution had on the very early church with the Muslim expansion of the seventh and eighth centuries. In the case of the early church, despite fierce opposition it continued to grow. By the seventh century, the church had all but lost its earlier spiritual vitality and was overcome.

It would, however, be wrong to assume that the Islamic occupation of former 'Christian' territory was a complete disaster. During those years, Islam presented a much more moderate face than is true of it in the present day. 'It far surpassed the West in intellectual achievement.'[3] The institution of the university came to the West from the Muslim world, with the first Muslim university being established in Cairo in 970. (Western universities did not begin to appear until the twelfth century.) University education was one component of the Renaissance (fourteenth and fifteenth centuries), which proved to be foundational to the Reformation.

The church in the early Middle Ages

NOTES

1 J. H. Merle d'Aubigné, *The Reformation in England*, vol. 1 (London: Banner of Truth Trust, 1963), p. 31.
2 The kingdom of the Franks consisted of much of modern-day France and western Germany.
3 N. R. Needham, *2000 Years of Christ's Power*, vol. 2 (Fearn/London: Christian Focus/Grace Publications Trust, 2016), p. 261 (p. 243 in 2000 edition).

The church's response to Islam

The iconoclastic[1] controversy

The act of the Muslims in taking over many parts of eastern Christendom seems to have led to what has been called the 'iconoclastic controversy'. Over several centuries, the use of icons in worship had steadily gained in popularity, especially in the eastern provinces of the Roman Empire. Toward the end of the sixth century and into the seventh, icons became the object of an officially encouraged cult, often implying a superstitious belief in their animation.

When the Islamic forces burned down churches, most of the icons in them would have been destroyed. What some Christians must have regarded as divine displeasure gave rise to strong opposition to the use of icons in worship. In 726, the Byzantine Emperor, Leo III, took a public stand against the perceived worship of icons, and in 730 their use was officially prohibited in the Eastern churches. But this reforming act did not last, since by 787 the use of images in worship was re-established. The dispute continued for more than five decades until 843, when icon veneration was finally and permanently restored in the Eastern churches. This event is still celebrated in the Eastern Orthodox Church as the 'Feast of Orthodoxy'. One of the arguments which carried weight in the decision to continue using icons was that the 'royal road of tradition' indicated that icons were beneficial. Tradition clearly trumped Scripture in the matter. In deciding thus, the Eastern churches turned away from a path towards reformation and were consequently largely bypassed when God 'awoke' the western part of the Church during the Reformation.

The church's response to Islam

The intensity of feeling provoked by the iconoclastic controversy can be illustrated by an incident which took place when the Byzantine Emperor, Leo III, gave orders for his soldiers to pull down a gigantic golden statue of Christ on the palace gate of Constantinople. 'A mob of enraged women seized the officer in charge and beat him to death with mops and kitchen tools.'[2] (Such an event is reminiscent of the murder of PC Blakelock in London in 1985.)

Such a murderous frenzy shows deep devotion to icons. In the case cited, the image of Christ was not merely an aid to true worship, but was, in fact, nothing less than an idol.

The Holy Roman Empire

In the seventh century, the papacy was in its infancy, and the popes were trying to stamp their authority on the church. The loss of so much of Christendom to the Muslim invaders must therefore have seemed a real setback. In addition, after the fall of Rome in 476 when the western part of the empire began to fragment, the continuation of the eastern section of the empire with its own emperors would have acted as a spur to successive popes to attempt to restore the empire in the West. This finally came to fruition on Christmas Day 800, when the Pope, Leo III, crowned Charles (Charlemagne), king of the Franks, in Rome as the first emperor of what was later called the 'Holy Roman Empire'. Leo claimed that this new empire, not that centred on Constantinople, was the true successor to Constantine and the 'Christian' Roman Empire in the West.

The Holy Roman Empire was more of a political idea than a powerful reality. It was, however, of use to successive popes to help consolidate their authority in northern Europe. Despite weakness at times, during the Middle Ages the empire was, along with the papacy, the most important institution of Western Europe. At its greatest extent it included Germany, the Netherlands, Bohemia, Austria, Switzerland, much of Italy, and parts of eastern France.

Chapter 6

Inevitably there was conflict between popes and emperors, mainly caused by papal ambition. Successive popes and emperors often quarrelled, each vying with the other for supremacy. During the late Middle Ages these quarrels went on for centuries. One rather bizarre example of the struggle between popes and emperors is that of Emperor Henry IV in the late eleventh century. Because Henry had refused to submit to the Pope (Gregory VII), all the churches in the Empire were closed, causing great consternation among lower-ranking officials. Henry was eventually persuaded to cross the Alps in midwinter with his wife and child. Arriving at the Pope's residence in Tuscany, he was forced to wait barefoot in the snow for three successive days. On the fourth day, the Pope condescended to give him an audience, at which Henry expressed abject sorrow and contrition. Only this act of servile grovelling succeeded in lifting the ban and permitting churches to be reopened. What a contrast between the Pope's haughty attitude and the meekness and humility of Christ!

The Crusades

For the best part of five hundred years, the Muslim rulers of Palestine had permitted Christian pilgrims to visit the 'holy' sites there. (These 'sacred' sites had been designated during the early fourth century as 'authentic' by Helena, mother of Constantine the Great.)

During the latter part of the eleventh century, however, the Turks were beginning to dominate the Middle East and took over the jurisdiction of Palestine. Unlike the Arabian Muslims, the Turkish authorities regarded 'Christian' pilgrims as an unwarranted intrusion into Muslim territory and made life increasingly difficult for any who wished to visit the Holy Land. They behaved harshly and oppressively towards visiting Christians, making pilgrimage almost impossible for all but the very resolute.

The Crusades were in direct response to this Turkish obstruction of Christian pilgrims. They were a series of military expeditions to the Middle East by Western Catholics, inspired and 'blessed' by the church, with the

The church's response to Islam

aim of recapturing the Holy Land from the Muslims. Direct impetus was given to the First Crusade in a famous sermon by Pope Urban II in 1095. Exaggerating the recent anti-Christian acts of the Muslims, Urban exhorted Christendom to go to war, particularly to recover the site of the Holy Sepulchre in Jerusalem. The battle cry of the Christians, he urged, should be *Deus vult* (God wills it). The Crusaders took their name from the crosses that were distributed at this meeting. It is estimated that, during the succeeding months, between 60,000 and 100,000 heeded the Pope's call and took up the cause of the First Crusade. The factors that contributed to this enthusiastic response were not, however, always related to religious devotion. The desire to increase Western influence and increase trade in the East were also significant motives. A general awakening to the lure of travel and adventure was also present.

Four main crusades were undertaken over the next hundred years, each lasting approximately two to four years. Overall, despite temporary victories, they were an abysmal failure and the total death toll ran into millions. All the territory originally under Muslim control eventually reverted to Muslim rule. The Crusades also introduced a new note of cruelty and religious intolerance into Christian/Muslim relations. In the First Crusade, the entire population of Jerusalem was massacred by the Crusader armies. Not surprisingly, such acts as these have had a negative influence on Muslim thinking right up to the present day and have resulted in Muslims being resistant to the gospel.

NOTES

1 For the purposes of this book, an iconoclast is someone who destroys a religious image or painting. Details of the iconoclastic controversy can be found in N. R. Needham's *2000 Years of Christ's Power*, vol. 2 (Fearn/London: Christian Focus/Grace Publications Trust, 2016), chapter 3, section 3.
2 Needham, *2000 Years* (2016 edition), vol. 2, p. 103 (p. 93 in the 2000 edition).

Medieval dissent

In chapter 5 we considered the history of the primitive church in Britain during the early part of the Middle Ages. We briefly traced the missionary endeavours of Patrick, Columba and Columbanus, in Ireland, north-west England, Wales and even further afield to Europe. We observed, too, that the more biblically-based Celtic Christianity arose independently from Roman Catholic influence, and remained independent until the end of the seventh century. By that time, the truer gospel light those men had embraced had all but been extinguished in Britain. Patrick, Columba and Columbanus are now all considered by the Roman Catholic Church to be 'saints', despite their independence from and opposition to the teachings of Rome. The Roman Catholic histories of them have had to be rewritten in order to achieve canonisation.

Even with the disappearance of the more biblically-based Christianity of the Celtic Church, God had not forgotten his cause and still had great future purposes for the British people. During the 'dark ages' when ignorance, superstition, and the domination of Rome were predominant, God raised up a series of men, all of whom in their own way became stepping stones to the Reformation of the sixteenth century.

Alfred the Great, king of Wessex (871–899), encouraged the study of the Scriptures and translated part of the Psalms into Anglo-Saxon before his premature death in the late ninth century. He is reported as revising English law to be based on the principles of the Mosaic Law in the Old Testament.

William the Conqueror, too, had no sooner set foot in England in 1066 than he began to make changes in the church without the permission of the Pope. He replaced the Archbishop of Canterbury and passed a law which allowed priests to marry. William may not have acted from the highest motives, but there was no interference from Rome during his reign.

Medieval dissent

In 1215, the English barons forced King John to sign Magna Carta, which, among other things, upheld the liberties of the English people against any intervention from Rome. Admittedly John soon capitulated to Rome,[1] but Magna Carta was yet another milestone on the road leading to the reformation of the church.

Robert Grosseteste, Bishop of Lincoln, followed in the mid thirteenth century. He asserted the authority of Scripture over the authority of the church. He was a powerful preacher in English, who expected people to come to hear the Word of God. 'The work of a priest is not giving people the mass, but preaching the living truth,'[2] he said. When he died he was acclaimed as 'a searcher of the Scriptures, an adversary of the Pope, and a despiser of the Romans'.[3]

Archbishop Bradwardine and Edward III (late thirteenth and early fourteenth centuries) both continued the opposition to Rome. Bradwardine encouraged a purer faith to be taught in the church, while Edward passed laws which prevented any ecclesiastical appointments being made by foreigners and stemmed the flow of money out of the country to line the coffers of the Vatican.

Italian dissent

From the foothills of the Alps in north-west Italy, the plain of Lombardy extends south-eastwards for some two hundred miles. Two of its main towns are Milan and Turin. During the fourth century and beyond, the diocese of Milan included the Lombardy plain, the Alps of Piedmont (or Cottian Alps), and the southernmost provinces of France. For many centuries, this region was noted for the independence of its churches. In 555, Pope Pelagius I complained that, 'the Bishops of Milan do not come to Rome for ordination'.[4] There is solid evidence from the writings of church leaders of this region, that the evangelical faith of Ambrose, under whose ministry Augustine was converted, continued for many hundreds of years. In the ninth century, one of the most notable of these 'champions of

A Beginner's Guide to Church History **47**

Chapter 7

the truth' was Claudius, Bishop of Milan. Claudius wrote commentaries on the Gospels, and expositions on almost all the letters of Paul and on some Old Testament books. Some of the key doctrines which Claudius maintained were:

- Jesus Christ alone is the head of the church.
- Peter was not superior to the other apostles.
- Faith alone, not human merit, saves us.
- Scripture, not tradition, is to be our authority.
- We should not pray for the dead.
- Relics are of no value and should be re-interred.
- The Lord's Supper is a memorial of Christ—there is no change in the elements during the communion service.
- Use of images in worship is a violation of the second commandment.

Claudius' writings on many of the above points are extensive and leave us in no doubt as to his beliefs. All this shows that evangelical light was still shining in the churches of that region, well after many other sections of Western Christendom had been brought under the authority and increasingly unbiblical teachings of the Roman Church. Claudius' influence continued in the region for some two hundred years after his death, as it was not until 1059 that the churches of Lombardy finally succumbed to the jurisdiction of Rome.[5] It seems very likely that there is a direct link between the remnant of the eleventh century evangelical churches of Lombardy and the Waldensians who lived in the more mountainous region at the foot of the Alps, from the twelfth century onwards. We shall now turn our attention to this intriguing group of believers.

The Waldensians

Although they existed before him, the Waldensians take their name from Peter Waldo, a wealthy merchant who came from Lyons, on the French side of the Cottian Alps. In 1174, he renounced his wealth and became a travelling preacher. Others joined his group, and they became known as the 'Poor Men of Lyons'. They soon ran into problems with the established church for two reasons: they had no formal training as clergy, and they were handing out Bibles in the vernacular (instead of Latin). Church officials told Peter Waldo and his associates to stop preaching without the consent of the local clergy.

But the Waldensians continued to preach their message of repentance and also encouraged the personal study of the Scriptures (in one's own language). The Waldensians loved the Bible and insisted that it should be their sole authority. At the same time, they publicly criticized the corruption of the Roman Catholic clergy. The Waldensians rejected many of the superstitious traditions of Catholicism, including prayers for the dead, holy water, indulgences and the doctrine of Purgatory. The Communion, they said, was a memorial of Christ's death, not a sacrifice. They did not follow the church's calendar concerning days of fasting, and they refused to bow before altars, venerate saints, or treat 'holy' bread as holy. The rejection of so much fundamental Catholic teaching meant that the Waldensians were perceived as launching a pre-Reformation reform movement.

The order and practice of these believers is instructive. They were the first to possess a translation of the complete New Testament in their own language, Romaunt, which was the common language of southern Europe from the eighth to the fourteenth centuries. In contrast to the elaborately adorned copies of the Latin Vulgate Scriptures, these Romaunt New Testaments were small, plain and portable. Trainee pastors were required to memorize and accurately recite whole Gospels and Epistles. They transcribed their own portions for distribution. Their pastors preached, visited the sick and catechized[6] the young. All the pastors met annually in a Synod with an equal number of laymen, and appointed a single moderator from among their number. They were missionary-minded and travelled in twos across Europe as merchants or pedlars, selling items

Chapter 7

not easily available, such as silks and jewellery. While making these sales to a household they would often offer their customers free portions of Scripture and explain them if asked.

The Waldensians' back-to-the-Bible approach appealed to many, and the movement quickly spread to Spain, northern France, Flanders, Germany, southern Italy, and even Poland and Hungary. But its greatest effect was felt in southern France. The people of this region who had embraced the gospel are sometimes referred to as the Albigenses. There also seems to be a link with refugees, called Cathars, fleeing earlier persecutions from Eastern Orthodox Churches. The term Cathar (Greek for 'pure one') was at that time a general term in Eastern Orthodoxy for heretics.

The Catholic Church did not take kindly to the Waldensians' missionary zeal and call for reform. In 1181 the Archbishop of Lyons excommunicated them. Three years later, Pope Innocent III declared them to be heretics, and in 1215 an anathema or formal curse was pronounced against Waldensian doctrine. Just a few years prior to this anathema, Innocent had promoted a crusade against the Albigenses. At least 50,000 crusaders were involved in a scorched earth policy against these 'heretical' inhabitants of southern France. The end result was that the whole region, which had had fruitful farmland and flourishing cities, and contained an orderly, virtuous population, now lay as a blackened and silent desert.[7] To his shame, once these lands had been purged of 'heresy', they came under the control of the English nobleman, Simon de Montfort, who had been one of the crusaders.

Persecution against the rest of the Waldensians increased in the 1230s and lasted, on and off, for more than three hundred years. In some areas they faced the death penalty if they refused to recant, and the recently-established Inquisition began actively seeking the leaders of the various Waldensian groups. The Waldensians went underground, and many groups retreated into remote areas in the Alps in order to survive.

These persecutions, and others which were to follow, mark a reinstatement of the kind of violent persecution of the people of God which had died out in the fourth century.

NOTES

1. See J. H. Merle d'Aubigné, *The Reformation in England*, vol. 1 (London: Banner of Truth Trust, 1963), pp. 70–71.
2. N. R. Needham, *2000 Years of Christ's Power*, vol. 2, (Fearn/London: Christian Focus/Grace Publications Trust, 2016), p. 278 (p. 259 in the 2000 edition).
3. J. H. Merle d'Aubigné, *The Reformation in England*, vol. 1 (London: Banner of Truth Trust, 1963), p. 74.
4. J. A. Wylie, *History of Protestantism*, vol. 1 (London: Cassell and Company, n.d.), p. 19.
5. Wylie, *History*, vol. 1, p. 23.
6. Catechising is a question-and-answer method of teaching children.
7. Wylie, *History*, vol. 1, p. 37.

First streaks of dawn

John Wycliffe—morning star of the Reformation

John Wycliffe was born about 1329 near Richmond in Yorkshire. Like many other young men of his day, he went up to Oxford to study, probably at the age of 14. In 1348, a terrible plague, which had devastated Asia and Europe, appeared in England. It awoke fears of the Day of Judgement in the heart of Wycliffe, then around 19 years of age, and he called upon God to show him the path he ought to follow. He found the answer in the Scriptures, which he then resolved to make known to others also.

Wycliffe's academic career was a brilliant one. He came to be known as 'the Flower of Oxford'. In 1360 he was elected as Master of Balliol College and about 1365 he took up the post of Warden of Canterbury Hall. He began, at this time, to teach and preach the Christian faith more boldly. During the week he would demonstrate to the learned, what he intended to preach on the Sunday. He accused the clergy of having banished the Scriptures and insisted that the authority of the Word of God should be re-established in the church.

In the mid 1370s, debates took place in Parliament to decide whether or not tribute (a special tax) should be paid to the Pope. The Vatican had previously attempted to levy this money from King John, but it had never been paid. Partly due to Wycliffe's influence, a motion was passed in Parliament to the effect that the Pope had no right to this tribute.

About this time, Wycliffe was appointed as rector of Lutterworth, and in this capacity he began to speak out more boldly on contemporary issues.

First streaks of dawn

Some of his statements alarmed the clergy, and on two separate occasions he was summoned to answer for his views. On both occasions, little was achieved and the clergy were unable to muzzle the Reformer.

Up until now, Wycliffe had been much involved in politics, but the thrust of his later years was to be spent primarily on spiritual matters. Three particular areas deserve notice:

(a) The Wycliffe Preachers (Lollards)

Wycliffe had seen the 'begging friars' preaching all over the country, and he conceived the idea of sending out true gospel preachers countrywide. After their sermons, the Wycliffe preachers, or Lollards, did not retire to the alehouses or gaming tables as the friars usually did. Instead, they visited the sick, the poor, and the aged, giving them what help they could.[1]

John Wycliffe and the Lollard preachers

Chapter 8

The clergy became alarmed at this move and had a law passed to have Lollard preachers committed to prison. But they were largely unsuccessful, because often no sooner had the officials come to arrest them, than a crowd of armed men would surround them and no action could be taken.

(b) Translation of the Bible

For many years we can see in the life of Wycliffe a growing knowledge of and submission to the Word of God. He clearly desired that others should be able to read and understand for themselves the truth which up till now had been hidden from all but the well-educated. By 1379, he had been working on the translation of the Scriptures into English for at least a decade.

Wycliffe was not a Greek or Hebrew scholar, and manuscripts in these languages were scarce. But his Latin was second to none, and so he was able to translate from the Latin Vulgate. It was sometime between 1380 and 1384 that the work was completed. He was assisted in some of it by other scholars, but according to the traditional view most of the work was his. As soon as it was finished, the work of copying began, for there was no printing press in those times. Altogether, several hundred copies were made—no mean achievement for those times! It is thought that as many as 250 copies survive to this day: one was sold at auction in 2016 for more than $1.5 million.

(c) The doctrine of the mass

Until quite late in his life, Wycliffe had accepted the doctrine of transubstantiation—that the bread and wine are changed into the body and blood of Christ when the priest has consecrated them. By 1378, he came to see the error of this teaching. In typical fashion he did not keep his new-found beliefs to himself, but began to preach and teach them with characteristic vigour. The inevitable storm broke. Even his friends began to desert him. Many could go along with his denunciation of the Pope, but few could follow him in this path.

First streaks of dawn

Two other attempts were made to silence the Reformer; both were unsuccessful, and after suffering a stroke on 29 December 1384, John Wycliffe quietly passed into eternity on the last day of that year.

The Lollard preachers continued for many years after Wycliffe's death, but the increasing severity of persecution eventually drove them underground. In the early 1400s, laws were passed in England to make the possession of any part of the Bible in English a capital offence, punishable with death by burning at the stake. To their shame, the English clergy were behind the enactment of this brutal legislation.[2]

Gospel light in Bohemia—John Huss

There is no direct link between Wycliffe and Luther, but there is however an intermediate link in the person of John Huss, so now we turn our attention to this continental champion of the faith.

John Huss came from the central European country of Bohemia (in the modern-day Czech Republic), whose capital is Prague. Christianity did not come to Bohemia until about the eighth century, and even then early converts were very nominal: so much so, that in the ninth century the king of Moravia (a neighbouring country to Bohemia) requested that the Scriptures be translated into the Slavonic language.

The result of this was that a large number of people were converted. Subsequently, for some two hundred years the Bohemians were able to enjoy worship and read the Scriptures in their own tongue. But by the late eleventh

Statue of Jan Hus (John Huss) in Husinec, in the South Bohemian Region of the Czech Republic

A Beginner's Guide to Church History 55

Chapter 8

century, by order of the Pope, the Latin service was reintroduced into the churches and Slavonic Bibles banned. Evangelical influences were, however, not altogether lost, for around that time a number of Waldensian refugees came to the country, fleeing from persecution in their homeland in the mountains of northern Italy. These people were zealous evangelists, not in public, but teaching in private houses. As a result, they had kept alive a purer faith than was taught and practised by Rome. Another factor which helped to prevent Bohemia from falling into total spiritual darkness was that in some churches, protected by local nobility, worship was still continued in the Slavonic language.

In the mid fourteenth century, Charles, king of Bohemia, was also elected as the Emperor of the 'Holy Roman Empire' (see chapter 6). One of his achievements was to set up the University of Prague, with the aim of making it equal in learning with Paris and Oxford. Charles' son and successor was the famed king Wenceslaus, who forged a link with England by arranging the marriage of his sister Anne to king Richard II. Anne was a godly woman, who loved the Word of God and encouraged the writings of John Wycliffe to be brought into Bohemia. The stage had thus been set for the appearance of God's man for the hour, John Huss.

While all these things were occurring, John Huss was growing up as a young peasant lad in the village of Husinec, from which he seems to have taken his name. John Huss's father died when he was quite young, and his mother was assisted in the cost of his education by a rich nobleman. Huss did not disappoint his mother or their rich patron. By the time he was thirty-four, he had been appointed Rector of the University of Prague, one of the highest academic attainments possible. Around this time an event occurred which was to be a turning point in his life. In Prague, some ten years earlier, Bethlehem Chapel had been opened specifically for the preaching of God's word in the Slavonic language. In 1402 Huss was appointed its preacher. He began to speak out against the many sins and vices of his day, so much so that he seemed to be a kind of conscience for the nation. He not only studied the Scriptures but also, at this time, the writings of John Wycliffe. It seems as though it was in the course of preparation and delivery of these sermons that the preacher himself became spiritually awakened.

It was not long before Huss's preaching in Prague gained the attention of the Pope, particularly when Huss began to speak out against the sale of indulgences. Firstly the books of John Wycliffe were collected and burned publicly in Prague. Then Huss himself was summoned to Rome. He was advised not to go, so the Pope condemned him, in absentia, and placed the city of Prague under interdict. This meant that the churches were closed, the altar lights were put out and the images were covered over with sackcloth. Huss was forced to withdraw from Prague to his native town of Husinec. He was unable to preach in Prague, but he spent much of his time travelling around the country, preaching in other towns and villages. Great crowds heard him gladly. During this period, Huss came to a clearer understanding of the doctrine of the church, and wrote a treatise on the subject called *On the Church*. A hundred years later, this book proved to be a great help to Luther.

Clearly the Church of Rome could not tolerate this state of affairs for long; but there was a fundamental problem which prevented decisive and united action. There were at that time still three popes, one in Italy, one in Spain and one in France. Before any effective move could be made against the reform movement this division had to be healed. The new Emperor, Sigismund, also king of Bohemia, had the bright idea of calling a church council, and thus it was that in 1414 the Council of Constance was convened.

The Council was a very splendid affair. As well as the emperor, it included other kings and nobles from all over Europe, to say nothing of cardinals, archbishops, bishops and priests, all with an entourage corresponding to their rank. It has been estimated that the city of Constance had an influx of around 100,000 people. The first business of the Council was to settle

Chapter 8

the question of the Pope. In the event, all three popes were deposed and a new one elected.

The Council then turned its attention to the Reformer. John Huss had only agreed to come to the Council on the basis of a 'safe-conduct' granted to him by the emperor, Sigismund. But he had not been in the city for more than a few weeks when he was arrested and thrown into prison. He was confined for six months in a damp, unhealthy dungeon situated on the banks of the river Rhine, next to where the main town sewer emptied into the river. At his first appearance, Huss was unable to speak in his own defence, because he was shouted down by many of the clerics opposed to him. It soon became clear that his condemnation had been predetermined, and only a full recantation of all those beliefs which in any way conflicted with the teaching of the Church would save him. He was unwilling to recant, so eventually, in July 1415, he was sentenced to death by burning.

So ended the life of John Huss. When finally fastened to the stake, he is said to have uttered these memorable and prophetic words: 'It is thus that you silence the goose, but a hundred years hence there will arise a swan whose singing you will not be able to silence.'[3]

Huss's ideas were, in some ways, less advanced than those of Wycliffe. For instance, he never came to a clear understanding of the doctrine of the Lord's Supper. His view was probably similar to Luther's (see note 9, chapter 10), whereas Wycliffe had come to see that transubstantiation was not according to Scripture. On the other hand, Huss did begin a reform movement among the population of Bohemia which continued for several decades after his death and which, for a while, successfully challenged the power of the Roman Church. As with Wycliffe and Luther, the touchstone of his understanding was the Scriptures. He asserted the right of every man to make his own decisions on the basis of the Bible and to find salvation in Christ alone.

NOTES

1 J. H. Merle d'Aubigné, *The Reformation in England*, vol. 1 (London: Banner of Truth Trust, 1963), p. 86.
2 d'Aubigné, vol. 1, p. 103.
3 J. A. Wylie, *History of Protestantism*, vol. 1 (London: Cassell and Company, n.d.), p. 164.

The darkness deepens but God prepares his way

So far in this history we have arrived at the early fifteenth century and the funeral pyre of the Bohemian 'Reformer' John Huss in 1415. The Council of Constance, which had condemned Huss without a proper hearing, also decreed John Wycliffe to be a heretic and his bones were dug up and ceremoniously burned. Any in England who were found in possession of even part of Wycliffe's translation of the Bible, could now face being burned at the stake. Such persecution of the 'Lollards'[1] continued for the next hundred years and was only interrupted by the emergence of the Reformation. The Roman Catholic Church had become as much a persecutor of the people of God as the earlier Roman emperors had been. The 'holy office' of the Inquisition had been set up by Pope Innocent III in the early thirteenth century, and over the next few hundred years much blood would flow as a result of its activities. 'Drunk with ... the blood of those who bore testimony to Jesus' (Rev. 17:6, NIV) is surely a fitting epithet for the perpetrator of all these atrocities. During the late Middle Ages, the Inquisition would become the most feared institution in society. A twentieth-century equivalent is the KGB in pre-1990s Soviet Russia.

The invention of printing

But, as is always the case, even in the darkest times God was at work. Even as John Huss was breathing his last, a young lad was growing up in Germany who would produce an invention that would change the world. I refer to Johann Gutenberg, the inventor of the printing press which used moveable type, consisting of all the letters of the alphabet, individually

The darkness deepens but God prepares his way

cast in lead. Gutenberg was a silversmith by profession and knew how to make small accurate metal castings. The lead type was assembled in the appropriate order for the words required, then a whole page of assembled type was clamped together and mounted in the press. The design of his first press was based upon those used for making wine or cheese. The first documents he printed were, ironically, indulgence 'certificates'. His ink was made from soot, turpentine and walnut oil.[2] His masterpiece

Replica of Gutenberg's printing press

was the printing of the complete Bible in Latin in 1453–54. This had a print run of only 180 copies. Improvements to the design of printing presses took place over the next few decades until by 1500 a single press could produce 3600 book pages in a working day. By that time there were 250 presses spread across Europe. The works of Erasmus and Luther ran to hundreds of thousands of copies during their lifetime.[3] The production of Bibles fuelled literacy, as there was a real hunger to read God's Word, so long withheld from the rank and file.

The fall of Constantinople

1453 was a crucial year for another reason. It was the year in which Constantinople finally fell to Turkish advance, marking the end of the Byzantine Empire. The significance of this was that classical scholars in Latin, Greek and Hebrew from that city, as they saw imminent destruction approaching, decided to move both themselves and many valuable ancient

Chapter 9

documents into Europe. Many of these refugee scholars settled in northern Italy. One in particular, named John Bessarion, formed schools to teach Greek. He gathered a large collection of Greek manuscripts, which were later donated to the city of Venice. The appearance in the West of all this ancient literature, which had been 'locked away' in the libraries of the Eastern empire for nearly a thousand years, was undoubtedly one of the most important factors behind what is referred to as the Renaissance.

The Renaissance (or 'rebirth') was a historical movement which started in the late fourteenth century and continued until the seventeenth. It was one of those movements in history where it is difficult to determine why it occurred. Like *Glasnost* and *Perestroika* in late twentieth-century Russia, it just appeared, seemingly from nowhere. Many think of the Renaissance mainly in terms of art and music, where there were certainly great changes; but the Renaissance also marked a shift in philosophical and theological thought, away from the prevailing medieval mind-set, back to classical Greek and Latin studies. 'Back to the sources' was the slogan of the times. With printed copies now becoming readily available, scholars did not need to have access to original manuscripts, but could obtain copies for themselves. From the church's point of view, the most important components of this treasury of literature were significant numbers of Greek and Hebrew biblical manuscripts. There was also now, among other things, a clamour to learn Greek and Hebrew so as to be able to read and analyse this literature.

Erasmus and the Greek New Testament

The person to whom the church is particularly indebted for making the Greek New Testament available is Desiderius Erasmus (his chosen pseudonym, meaning 'pleasing' and 'longing'). Having mastered Greek as well as Latin, Erasmus gathered together as many Greek manuscripts as he could and produced his Greek New Testament. One of the significant features of this volume was that it contained not only the complete Greek text but also, in parallel with the Greek, both Jerome's Latin Vulgate version and Erasmus' own Latin translation. This had the effect of exposing serious flaws in vital doctrines of Jerome's version, which had misled the church for a thousand years. In particular, the error of medieval works-based salvation was exposed. Consequently, the faith-alone, grace-alone theological understanding which the Reformers grasped was able to shine out. As a result, millions were led out of spiritual darkness into the light and liberty of the truth of the gospel.

The ready availability of Erasmus' Greek New Testament was foundational to the translation of the Scriptures into all the major European languages during the sixteenth century. By the end of the century, Bibles were available in these languages, even where the Reformation had been slow to reach or where dominant Catholic regimes had endeavoured to suppress it.

NOTES

1 A name given to followers of Wycliffe's teachings.
2 C. P. Hallihan, *The Protestant Reformation* (London: Trinitarian Bible Society, 2017), p. 9.
3 Hallihan, *The Protestant Reformation*, p. 10.

A great light: the sixteenth century Reformation

If there is a single phrase which sums up the massive change which occurred in sixteenth century Europe, it is the motto of the city of Geneva—*post tenebras lux* (after darkness, light). Some consider the Reformation to be the greatest revival of faith since the days of the apostles. If that is the case, two of the first questions which come to mind are: 'How did this change take place?' and 'When did it all begin?' Surprisingly, some of the leading players were reluctant heroes.

A troubled monk

The one act which can be considered as marking the beginning of the Reformation was when the German monk, Martin Luther, nailed his '95 Theses' to the door of the castle church in Wittenberg in Saxony (central Germany). Space does not allow details of Luther's early days, so we pick up the story with him in the Augustinian monastery in Erfurt, central Germany.

Luther had entered the monastery because of a vow he had made at a time of great distress. Like many before him, he thought that in the seclusion of the cloister he would be able to escape from the sin and evil in the outside world. But he was in for a rude shock and a wake-up to reality. The real problem was not so much the sin and evil outside, but the problem of his own sinful nature. As he sought relief in confession, fasting and afflicting his body, his struggles came to the notice of the head of the Augustinians in Saxony, Johann von Staupitz. The wise Staupitz recommended that he should not fast as much, that he should get more sleep and study God's Word. To help him do this, he arranged for

A great light: the sixteenth century Reformation

Luther to lecture in theology at the recently-opened university in nearby Wittenberg. And it was as Luther studied the Scriptures, particularly in the original languages, that the light of the gospel began to shine into his soul. It was understanding the true meaning of Romans 1:17, 'the just shall live by faith' (AV), which became 'the very gate of Paradise itself' to him.

The 95 theses

Luther might well have remained in comparative obscurity, were it not for a series of events which goaded him into action.

It happened like this. The Pope decided that he wanted to rebuild St Peter's in Rome. This required a huge amount of money, which was to be raised mainly by the sale of 'indulgences'. Now an indulgence was one of those means by which the church in those days had a spiritual hold over the hearts and minds of the faithful. For the payment of a suitable sum of money, a certain number of years could be taken off one's time in purgatory. According to Roman Catholic teaching, purgatory is a kind of halfway-house between this life and heaven, where one's sins would be gradually purged. You could also buy an indulgence for a dead relative. The man who was selling these indulgences throughout Germany was a monk from Leipzig called Tetzel. He was particularly good at making money by pulling at the heart-strings of the recently-bereaved. So bold was he that a jingle summed up the essence of his message as, 'When the coin in the coffer rings, the soul from purgatory springs!' And so Tetzel came into the vicinity of Wittenberg. Not everyone approved of this indulgence-monger, whose life was also a known scandal. Elector Frederick, Duke of Saxony, refused permission for him to enter Saxony. He came as near as he could to the border, about an hour's walk from Wittenberg, and crowds flocked from the town to hear him and buy his indulgences. Luther was appalled and stung into action. At first he began to warn his congregation in his sermons. But his opposition to Tetzel's

Chapter 10

indulgences soon came to the ears of Tetzel himself, who vigorously attacked the man who would dare to oppose his mission—approved as it was by the Pope.

What would Luther's response to this be? He was the kind of man who would not hesitate to take action if he felt he could do so. As well as a preacher, he was now Professor of Theology at the University of Wittenberg. This was his plan of action: he would spell out in some detail his objections to Tetzel and his sales of indulgences. He would do this by using the duly-appointed means, writing out his objections and pinning them to the church door, where other public notices were displayed. And he would do this to coincide with the very popular festival of All Saints which fell on 1 November. And so on the eve of All Saints Day, on 31 October 1517, Luther made his way to the Castle Church and nailed what are now referred to as the '95 theses' to the church door. Immediately people began to read the document, and great interest was aroused in it. It was soon copied, printed and distributed all over Germany, and within a matter of weeks it had been translated into the other major European languages. Even the Pope had a copy.

It is interesting to note that the theses were in fact quite mild in their tone. They were clearly against the doctrine of indulgences, but were very deferential towards the Pope. They were still far from the theological position which Luther eventually came to. And yet this was the document which sparked off the Reformation. At this point in time, no one could have guessed at the repercussions which this document would have. If anyone had asked him, Luther himself would not have had any idea as to what it would all lead to. As such, then, the events of 31 October 1517 were part of God's sovereign dealings with his church to bring it back to its biblical and apostolic roots. The Reformation was under way. There could now be no turning back. Luther has been rightly described as 'The monk who shook the world'.[1] We err greatly if we do not give thanks to God for him.

A great light: the sixteenth century Reformation

Rome's response

At first the Pope did nothing, perhaps hoping that it would be a storm in a teacup. But the stir that the 95 theses had produced across the whole of Europe meant that they and their author could not be ignored. Several attempts were then made to persuade Luther to change his mind. First of all, threats were made by one of the Pope's representatives, Cardinal Cajetan. Then pressure was applied to Frederick, Duke of Saxony, who was sympathetic to Luther's position. A public disputation was also held in Leipzig, at which the Reformer's position was strengthened. One of the main topics discussed was the human will. Did we have free will to choose to follow Christ or were our wills hopelessly enslaved to sin? In emphasising the bondage of the will, Luther showed a clear break with medieval scholastic thinking. Finally, on 15 June 1520, the Pope issued a 'bull'[2] condemning Luther and ordering that his writings be burned. In response, Luther burned the bull in public to show his contempt for its contents. We can see that by this point Luther had progressed from his position at the publication of the 95 theses, where he was very deferential to the Pope. He now realized that the Pope and all that he stood for were part of the problem.

Luther at the Diet of Worms

At that time, the newly-elected Holy Roman Emperor,[3] Charles V, convened a special council called a 'Diet'. It was decided to hold it in the city of Worms in south-west Germany, and Luther was summoned. Because of the threats against his life, he was advised not to go. But Luther was nothing if not courageous, so he set out from Wittenberg in early April 1521 and arrived in Worms on the sixteenth of that month. By this time Luther had become a kind of national spectacle, for the crowds who gathered in the streets when he entered Worms were as numerous as those who would gather to greet a conqueror returning from victory. It has to be added that many in the crowds were hostile to this monk who had had

Chapter 10

the temerity to stand up and oppose both church and Pope. Indeed, the next day when he and his supporters attempted to go from their lodgings to the Diet, the streets were so thronged that they only managed to reach the conference hall with great difficulty.

Luther at the Diet of Worms

By any standards the Diet was a brilliant and imposing assembly. There were the emperor, his electors, dukes, margraves, archbishops, bishops, abbots, ambassadors and deputies of free cities. In all there were 206 people representing most of Europe and the whole of the church. On a table, all Luther's writings were displayed and he was asked two questions: Were they his writings, and would he retract those doctrines in them which were contrary to the teachings of the church? Luther examined the books and acknowledged that he was their author. He requested more time to consider the second question, and the proceedings were adjourned until the following day. In preparation, Luther spent time in prayer, and we are fortunate enough to have part of that prayer recorded by one of his friends:

A great light: the sixteenth century Reformation

O God, my God, be with me and protect me against the enemies of the world. Thou must do it, Thou alone, for in me is no strength. It is Thy cause, O God, not mine. On Thee I rely, not on man, for that would be in vain. O God, dost Thou not hear? Do not hide Thy face from me. Thou hast called me, now be my stay. I ask it in the Name of Thy Son, Jesus Christ, my protector, my shield and my defence.[4]

The next day, 18 April 1521, was the greatest day in Luther's life and described by one writer as 'one of the sublimest scenes which earth has ever witnessed'. The question was put to him again as to whether or not he would withdraw his writings. His reply, first made in Latin and then the whole repeated in German, lasted for about two hours. It ended with these immortal words:

Unless I am convinced by testimonies of the Scriptures or by clear arguments that I am in error—for popes and councils have often erred and contradicted themselves—I cannot withdraw, for I am subject to the Scriptures I have quoted; my conscience is captive to the Word of God. It is unsafe to do anything against one's conscience. Here I stand; I cannot do otherwise. So help me God.[5]

To put it mildly, the Diet was not impressed. Because he had been granted a safe conduct by the emperor, Luther was allowed to leave Worms unmolested on 25 April. A few days later, however, the Diet agreed that he should be placed under the 'Ban of the Empire',[6] so that any who harboured or sheltered him could be liable to a charge of high treason against the emperor.

Capture and imprisonment

Unbeknown to Luther, he was in grave danger. After a few days travelling, he and his companions entered the forest of Thuringia. Suddenly they were surrounded by a group of masked horsemen who seized Luther and carried him off into the forest. Under cover of darkness he was taken to a

Chapter 10

nearby castle, where he was told that he must adopt the garb of a knight and a new name and remain until it was safe for him to leave. Where was he? The next morning, as he looked out of the window, he realized that he was in the Wartburg Castle which overlooked the town of his upbringing, Eisenach. Frederick, Duke of Saxony, had organized Luther's capture and secret imprisonment. But to the world at large, he had vanished into thin air. Many in Wittenberg thought he was dead.

How was he to spend his time? Like the other Reformers, he realized that his task was hampered by the common people not being able to read the Scriptures in their own mother tongue. So he set about translating the New Testament into German, with the first pages being ready to print in just eleven weeks! By 1522 the complete New Testament was on sale in German shops for the equivalent of a craftsman's week's wage. Even at that price it sold like the proverbial hot cakes.

It is also interesting to note that while Luther was in the Wartburg Castle, events outside were working for the benefit of the Reformation. The Turkish Emperor Suleiman was advancing into eastern Europe. Meanwhile, war broke out between France and Spain, and the Emperor, Charles V, who was also king of Spain, had to return home. The Pope, Leo X, seemingly in good health, suddenly became ill and died so quickly that there was no time for him to be given the Last Rites. The new pope, Adrian VI, although no friend of the Reformation, was so different from Leo that those around him found it difficult to adjust to his

The title page of Luther's German translation of the Bible

A great light: the sixteenth century Reformation

attempts at reform. All these factors meant that for a while the spotlight was taken off Luther and the Reform movement at Wittenberg.

Luther returns to Wittenberg

All was not well, however, at this centre of the Reformation. There were some who were much more radical in their views than even Luther, and they wanted not only to dispense with the Pope and all the errors of the medieval church, but claimed special revelations from God. These extremists were threatening the whole cause of the Reformation.

As soon as Luther heard the news of these developments in Wittenberg, he decided to leave the security of his hilltop fortress and return there to stabilize matters. On his return he spent a whole week of discourses emphasising the need for caution in matters of reform and emphasizing the supreme authority of the Scriptures, which the German people would shortly have in their own language. The radicals were banished by the power of the Word, and matters were once more stabilized at Wittenberg.

An incomplete reformation

It seems, however, that these events at Wittenberg did influence Luther's thinking. Another factor which clearly had an influence on him was the Peasants' War. This was a movement which began in the south of Germany and, gaining momentum, threatened to engulf much of central Europe. Thomas Munzer, who had been one of the extremists in Luther's absence from Wittenberg, took a leading role. Luther at first attempted mediation, but neither the authorities nor the peasants took any notice of him. When all-out war broke out, he sided with the authorities. One hundred thousand were killed in the resulting conflict, but it hardly touched Saxony, where the Reformation had had its profoundest effect. The actions of Luther in breaking with the Church of Rome had clearly added impetus to this civil unrest. This must have hurt Luther deeply and

Chapter 10

it perhaps accounts for why after 1522 he made little further progress in reform, but retained some doctrines and practices which one would have thought he would have discarded.[7]

NOTES

1. C. J. Davey, *The Monk Who Shook the World* (Guildford: Lutterworth Press, 1974).
2. A 'bull' was an official papal written decree. It takes its name from the lead (Latin *bulla*) seal attached to the document.
3. The 'Holy Roman Empire' was created by the Pope in the year 800. The Empire consisted of the Germanic States and was ruled over by an elected Emperor. See chapter 6.
4. S. M. Houghton, *Sketches from Church History* (Edinburgh: Banner of Truth Trust, 1980), p. 89.
5. Houghton, *Sketches*, p. 89.
6. An imperial edict by which political rights and privileges were taken away.
7. Examples of doctrines and practices which Luther retained are: (i) The continued use of images in worship. (ii) The belief that the body and blood of Christ are mysteriously present in the sacrament of communion (consubstantiation).

God's Frenchman

Many people associate John Calvin with the city of Geneva, and rightly so. But he did not originate from there. He was born in 1509 in Noyon, Northern France. Like all his contemporaries he was raised a devout Roman Catholic, as that was the only version of Christianity on offer in those days. Space again prevents too much detail, so only some of the major events and turning points in his life are highlighted.

Calvin the loyal 'Catholic' student

It was while a student in Paris that John came into close contact with the new teaching of the Reformation. His cousin Robert was also studying in Paris at the time. In the evenings, John would go to his cousin's apartment to discuss subjects of common interest. Robert often pursued his studies far into the night, which had earned him the nickname of *Olivétan* ('midnight oil'). More importantly, Robert had been won over to the new teaching. John, however, was still a staunch supporter of the Roman Catholic Church and its practices. Their discussions often went on far into the night. There were two other events which influenced John's thinking at that time. One was the expulsion of the ageing Jacques Lefèvre from the University of Paris (the Sorbonne) for his publication of the New Testament in French. The other was the burning of an Augustinian monk, shortly after John's arrival in the capital.

Chapter 11

For a variety of reasons, Calvin left Paris to continue his studies elsewhere, but by 1533 he had returned. It was probably during his absence from the French capital that he was converted and became completely convinced that Reformation theology was more true to Scripture than what he had formerly believed.

Calvin escapes from Paris

By the time Calvin returned to Paris, his former friend Nicolas Cop had become the rector of the university and was due to give his inaugural lecture on All Saints Day. Cop had embraced the Reformed doctrines, and his discourse, though scholarly, was an exposition of Reformed truth. The authorities at the Sorbonne were furious and demanded that Cop appear for questioning. He felt sure that he could give a satisfactory answer, but taking the advice of a friend, he escaped from the city, and within two months had returned to the safety of his home town of Basle in Switzerland.

Calvin thought he was safe, but it was soon rumoured that he had had a hand in the writing of Cop's lecture. The bailiffs were sent to arrest him in his lodgings. Fortunately, he received prior warning and escaped into the narrow back street using a rope of twisted bed-curtains! He quickly ran to the house of a friend, borrowed a working man's disguise, and made his escape from the city. He had to leave his books and papers behind but he, himself, was free.

At this point in his life, the young Calvin was uncertain as to his life's work. His natural leanings were to study and write, but where to reside, where would it be safe? After brief visits to the south of France, Poitiers, and again Paris, an event occurred [1] which precipitated a violent persecution of all Protestants in the country. Calvin now knew that it was no longer safe to stay in France, so he and a friend set out for the German border. After a journey of some two hundred miles and considerable dangers on the way, they eventually reached Strasbourg. John, however, really wanted to settle in Basle to publish his second book. This was none other than the famous *Institutes of the Christian Religion*. In March 1536 the first edition, containing only six chapters, was on sale at the bookstalls. Its title page, in Latin, named the author as Jean Cauvin of Noyon. Its preface was addressed to King Francis I of France, to whom Calvin offered his book as a confession of faith. He was not even twenty-seven when it was first published.

After a brief visit to Northern Italy and another to Paris to help some of his immediate family escape, Calvin set out once more, this time for Strasbourg. But because the direct route was blocked by an army, he had to make a detour, and so, one evening in August 1536, he arrived at Geneva, travel-stained and hungry. He only intended to stay for the night, but God had other plans for him. He had barely finished his meal and was planning to have an early night, when the landlord knocked at the door of his room, introducing, 'Master William Farel with an urgent message'.

Farel, also a Frenchman, had been the first preacher of the Reformed faith in the area around Geneva. He had often preached in the open air and had been in danger many times, but now the citizens of Geneva had voted to become Protestant. Farel was experiencing considerable difficulty with the work of reform. On hearing that Calvin was staying overnight in the city, he seized the opportunity with both hands to request that Calvin should stay there to help in the work. Farel had read the *Institutes* and had realized the outstanding ability of its writer. At Farel's first request Calvin demurred. He insisted that he was not suited to public life but to be a scholar and write books. The debate continued for some time, with Calvin becoming increasingly concerned and begged his visitor to leave him in peace. But Farel would not go and in the end he persuaded the young Calvin to stay.[2] Thus John Calvin began his work at Geneva which, apart from a three-year break, lasted for twenty-eight years.

Chapter 11

Calvin the Reformer

At first Calvin was little known in the city, and although he had the task of a daily lecture at St Peter's, his audiences in that great auditorium were small.

Within a few weeks, however, an event occurred which thrust him into prominence. A public debate was scheduled to take place in Lausanne at the other end of Lake Geneva. Farel, Calvin and Viret, another of the leading Reformers, were all present. For three days Calvin remained silent, leaving the debating to Farel and Viret. On the fourth day, the Lord's Supper was the topic of discussion, and one of the Romanists made out a very strong case for the 'real presence'[3] in the sacrament, from the writings of the early Church Fathers. At this Calvin could hold his tongue no longer. He indicated his desire to take part and began to answer the Roman Catholic priest. He spoke without notes and quoted freely from the writings of Augustine, Chrysostom and others, inserting the passages which the priest had left out. Calvin also expounded the relevant Scriptures. The effect upon the debate was stunning, and one monk cried out that he had been in error all his life.

Calvin and the Libertines

The city of Geneva had embraced the teachings of the Reformation, but that did not mean that there was complete agreement on how the work of reforming the church should proceed. One aspect of 'Reformed' teaching was that a radically-changed life was an essential mark of true conversion. In Geneva at that time, a significant minority were unwilling to turn away from their old ways. They wanted the benefits of the gospel while still retaining the permissiveness of their previous lifestyle. The church leaders agreed to bar these 'Libertines' from the Lord's Supper. The day dawned for the new measures relating to the Lord's Supper to be implemented, but with the people in such a disorderly state the ministers decided that there would be no communion service on that day. At the afternoon service there was fighting even within the church, with the sound of small arms and the clash of swords! It was a miracle that there was no bloodshed.

The City Council was furious. Before the day was over they had set in motion the procedure to ban from the city Calvin, Farel and a blind pastor called Coraud. As they set out for Basle, Calvin reflected upon the recent events and was overcome with a great feeling of regret. 'I have been too hasty,' he confessed. 'I have tried to accomplish too much in too short a time and have shown myself unskilled in the work of the Lord.'[4] Truly a great man, he was willing to admit his part in the failure at Geneva.

Calvin in exile

The pastors from Geneva were kindly received at the church in Basle, which made provision for them. Soon afterwards, Farel received a call to Neuchatel, where he had formerly ministered. After some persuasion by Martin Bucer, Calvin agreed to minister to a growing congregation of French exiles in Basle. These refugees were delighted to hear the gospel preached in their own language. It was here that he prepared a hymn book which contained a selection of psalms, translated and set to music.

Meanwhile, back in Geneva, the situation had gone from bad to worse, and to compound it all, the Council received a letter from a Cardinal Sadoleto, seeking to woo them back to the bosom of Rome. Geneva was in difficulties. They had no intention of reverting to Catholicism, but who could answer the Cardinal's smooth and persuasive words? Only John Calvin. They wrote to him and asked him to reply to the letter. His response to Sadoleto was in Latin, containing 15,000 words. It was a brilliant defence of Protestantism, written in the same style which the Cardinal had used. Thus Rome's advances were repulsed.

It was while in exile that John's friends strongly advised him to marry. Two possible candidates were put forward, one of whom he deemed unsuitable because she was too rich, and when he met the other, he was

Chapter 11

not attracted to her. In the event, he fell in love with a member of his own congregation of French refugees, Idelette de Bure, a widow with two children. They were a devoted couple and despite poor health were constantly engaged in Christian work.

Calvin returns to Geneva

By the autumn of 1540 it was finally recognized by Geneva's Council that only John Calvin's firm hand could restore peace. So they invited him back. But he was busy taking part in a series of debates in Germany in an attempt by the emperor to bring Catholics and Protestants together. Even when these events were concluded, he hesitated. His whole nature shrank from it. He was far happier in his present role.

Many wrote to him advising him to return, but it was not until Farel wrote in February 1541 that he finally agreed. He was received back with great rejoicing. He was given a new gown lined with fur, and a new pulpit had been installed in St Peter's. In the summer of 1542 a baby son was born to the Calvins, but he lived only a few days. They had no other child, and his wife was never really well again.

Calvin spent the rest of his life in Geneva as a pastor and Reformer until his death in 1564. He preached through and wrote commentaries on many of the books of the Bible. Charles Haddon Spurgeon, the nineteenth-century Baptist preacher, considered his commentaries to be worth their weight in gold. During his time in the city, Geneva became a haven for the many thousands of refugees fleeing from persecution in neighbouring countries. Another notable achievement of Calvin's influence was undoubtedly the opening in 1559 of the Academy, the first Protestant university in the world. This project was financed by the citizens of Geneva, with even the poorest willingly making some contribution to the cost. It was formally opened just a few weeks before Calvin's fiftieth birthday.

There is much more that could be said about John Calvin. He wrote more than four thousand letters, some to church leaders and foreign heads of state. But it is perhaps the *Institutes*, whose final edition containing the eighty chapters we have today, and which was published in 1559, which have influenced the world the most.

NOTES

1. The 'night of the placards', when public notices were displayed all over Paris, with an irreverent attack on the Roman Catholic Mass.
2. E. M. Johnson, *Man of Geneva* (Edinburgh: Banner of Truth Trust, 1977), pp. 56–57.
3. The doctrine of the 'real presence' claims that, after consecration, the elements of bread and wine are changed to the actual body and blood of Christ.
4. Johnson, *Man of Geneva*, p. 85.

The English Reformation

The Reformation of the sixteenth century was undoubtedly the greatest and most notable work of God in his church since the days of the apostles. The Reformation changed the course of history: its influence on Western society has been incalculable. And that is where British Christianity comes in, for although the Reformation began on the continent, much preparatory work had already been done in Britain.[1] In addition, the effects of the Reformation were more profound on the British people than almost any other nation. In case it might be assumed that this is mere national pride, a quotation from the French historian Merle d'Aubigné in his book *The Reformation in England* underlines the point: 'There is no people among whom the Reformation has produced to the same degree that morality and order, that liberty, public spirit, and activity which are the very essence of a nation's greatness.'[2]

One of the most remarkable features of the Reformation was the way in which the recovery of Bible truth spread so rapidly throughout Europe. Discovered in Germany by Martin Luther, it was not long before its effect was being felt in England. Although Henry VIII is often regarded as the main character of the English Reformation, in fact he was often more of a hindrance than a help. His contribution was largely political, whereas the Reformation was not primarily a political event but a spiritual movement.

As in other European countries, there were many contributors to the Reformation, but in England one of the most important of them was William Tyndale. His contribution is foundational. Tyndale was born in Gloucestershire in the early 1490s and he went up to Magdalen College, Oxford, in 1505. In those days, the language of academic studies was Latin, so it is likely that this was the first foreign language that Tyndale learned.

The English Reformation

William Tyndale

He was later to supplement this with six others, including Hebrew, Greek and German.

After completing his studies at Oxford, Tyndale became tutor to the two young sons of the Walsh family in Little Sodbury Manor, back in his native Gloucestershire. It was while he was here that in an after-dinner discussion with a visiting cleric, he uttered the now famous words: 'If God spares my life, I will by God's grace see to it that the boy who drives the plough will know more of the Bible than thou dost.' This interaction seems to have been the catalyst which set Tyndale off on what was to be his life's work: the translation of the Bible into English.

At first he sought permission for this work from Cuthbert Tunstall, the Bishop of London, but soon found out that Tunstall had no sympathy for his project. So Tyndale ventured onto the continent, hoping to find somewhere there to carry out his work. At first he went to Wittenberg, where it is possible that he learned German from Katie, Luther's wife. By the mid 1520s he was ready to start printing and moved to Cologne. Unfortunately, one of the men who was employed by the printer, after having had too much to drink, let slip that they were printing the New Testament in English. Henry VIII's agents had the printer's premises raided and Tyndale was only able to escape with a few pages. He moved further up the Rhine to Worms to continue the work, and eventually by 1526 several thousand copies of the New Testament in English made their way into England. As soon as the Bishop of London found out

Chapter 12

about the publication, he had as many copies as possible seized and burned. The zealous bishop's actions did nothing to stem the flow of New Testaments, which, despite the danger of possessing one, were in great demand. They came into the country, mainly as printed sheets, hidden in other cargoes. Tyndale managed to produce two further revisions of his New Testament, but only two copies remain to this day.

Once the New Testament was available, Tyndale set to work on translating the Old Testament from the original Hebrew. By this time, Tyndale's competence in Hebrew was outstanding, so much so that some have taken

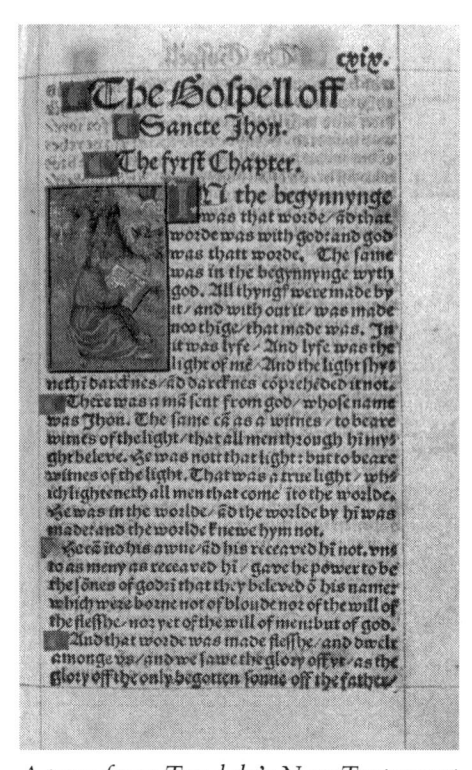

A page from Tyndale's New Testament

the view that stories of his ability in the language are apocryphal. There is, however, no justifiable reason for adopting this view. The circumstances in which Tyndale worked were often very discouraging. He had to be constantly on the move to avoid detection by Henry VIII's agents in Europe (one modern biographer's title is *God's Outlaw*).[3] Tyndale also lost some of his Old Testament manuscripts when a ship went down in the North Sea. But despite such setbacks, Tyndale was able to produce the Pentateuch by 1530 and then go on to translate the historical books of the Old Testament (Joshua to Esther). Eventually he was discovered in Antwerp and betrayed by someone he thought to be a friend. He was imprisoned in Vilvoorde Castle for more than a year and

The English Reformation

then burned in public in 1536. Mercifully, he was strangled before they lit the fire. Tyndale's dying words are reported to have been, 'Lord, open the king of England's eyes.' He was, of course, referring to Henry VIII, whose agents had achieved Tyndale's arrest and martyrdom. Although Henry would never have sanctioned the printing of Tyndale's Bible, Tyndale's prayer was answered a few years later when Henry issued a proclamation that an English Bible be placed in each church throughout his realm. Ironically, and unbeknown to Henry, that Bible was 90% Tyndale's work!

Although Henry VIII's break with Rome was an important act which helped the Reformation in England, two of Henry's wives were more instrumental in progressing the work of reform.

The first of these was Anne Boleyn. Anne received the secondary part of her education, from age 11 to 20, in the Netherlands and France, the latter part being under the supervision of her aunt, Margaret of Angoulême, who had embraced 'Reformed' teaching. Anne had her own New Testament in French, and by the time she returned from France in 1520 she was a supporter of the Reformation back in her homeland. Most of her family were Protestant, too. Anne was introduced to Henry's court during the lengthy Christmas celebrations of 1520/21 and became a lady-in-waiting to Queen Catherine. At that time she could have passed for a French courtier.

Much debate has taken place over the morality of Anne's involvement with Henry which eventually led to her becoming Queen. It would be inappropriate to cover the details of that debate within the scope of this book, but the following observations are offered:

1. Tudor marriage conventions were completely different from modern-day British law (quite apart from modern same-sex variants). A couple who had promised to each other, often with little more than joining hands, and then had physically consummated the marriage, were deemed married. Often any ceremony came later.

Chapter 12

2. There is clear evidence that Henry and Anne only consummated their marriage after a private ceremony in Dover on 14 November 1532.[4]
3. Both Anne and Henry believed (mistakenly) that his marriage to Catherine had been contrary to Scripture and invalid and that in consequence Henry was free to marry.

During her short reign, Anne supported and assisted the Protestant cause. Undoubtedly she was the catalyst in Henry's break with Rome. She worked alongside Archbishop Cranmer and among other things helped him in installing evangelical preachers in vacant 'livings'. She also brought her influence to bear in the appointment of three evangelical bishops in September 1535. She put pressure on Henry to protect evangelicals both at home and abroad. Anne was concerned about education and made generous donations to several educational establishments, including Oxford and Cambridge Universities. She promoted the trade in Bibles and evangelical books. She also sought to influence Parliament on behalf of the poor. She achieved much in her short time as queen. Anne was also the mother of Elizabeth, during whose forty-five-year reign the Protestant cause in England was greatly strengthened.

Anne's downfall was 'engineered' by Henry's Chancellor, Thomas Cromwell,[5] probably because he thought the Boleyns were becoming too powerful at court. Anne had disagreed with Cromwell over the dissolution of the monasteries. He wanted them and all their assets to be seized by the crown, whereas Anne was in favour of their reform, not destruction. It is generally acknowledged, even by her enemies, that the charges of adultery and incest brought against her were completely false. She was committed to the Tower in May 1536 and executed just a few weeks later. Cromwell's coup also included Anne's brother and several others deemed to be a hindrance to Cromwell's plans. On hearing of Anne's execution, Archbishop Cranmer burst into tears. By contrast, Henry, who was on a hunting party in Epping Forest when he heard the cannon signalling Anne's death, is reported as saying 'Ha, ha! the deed is done! Uncouple the hounds and away.'[6] Ironically, Thomas Cromwell met his end four years later, 'falsely convicted on a confusing mixture of rumour and innuendo'.[7]

The other woman who had a significant influence on the Protestant cause in England was Henry's sixth wife, Catherine Parr. Like Anne, as some at the time thought, she may have regarded marriage to Henry in a similar light to Esther's marriage to the pagan Persian king, Xerxes.[8] Both Anne and Catherine endeavoured to persuade their husband of the truth of Protestant Christianity. One of Catherine's main contributions to the Protestant cause was the supervision of part of the upbringing of both Elizabeth and Edward (Henry's son by his third wife, Jane Seymour). During Edward's short reign (1547–1553), significant strides forward were made in reforming the church. The ritual of the mass was replaced with the plain communion service. The sacraments of penance and the last rites of the dead were abolished. Purgatory was deemed to be a fiction and prayers for the dead were recognized as being of no value. Churches were stripped of their artefacts and priests no longer had to be celibate.

NOTES

1 John Wycliffe and the English Bible (see chapter 9).
2 J. H. Merle d'Aubigné, *The Reformation in England* (London: Banner of Truth Trust, 1963) vol. 1, pp. 23–24.
3 Brian Edwards, *God's Outlaw* (Welwyn: Evangelical Press, 1976).
4 Colin Hamer, *Anne Boleyn* (Leominster: Day One Publications, 2017), p. 74.
5 Not to be confused with Oliver Cromwell (see chapter 14).
6 d'Aubigné, *The Reformation in England*, vol. 2, p. 300.
7 Hamer, *Anne Boleyn*, p. 123.
8 The Old Testament book of Esther.

Rome's response: the Counter-Reformation

To the Church of Rome, the Protestant Reformation was a huge 'shock to the system'. What had started off as the complaints of a German monk had led to a massive defection from the 'mother church' all over Europe. What could be done to prevent the whole of Christendom from embracing the Protestant 'heresy'? The Pope's initial response was to call a Church Council at Trento in northern Italy: a series of three separate sessions between 1545 and 1563, now usually referred to as the Council of Trent. The decrees of the council, published at the completion of its deliberations, show that there was now no longer even a glimmer of hope of reconciliation between Protestant and Catholic. If anything, Rome had hardened her position.

Trent upheld the doctrines of transubstantiation, the necessary sacrificial ritual of the mass, the seven sacraments,[1] purgatory, indulgences and a celibate clergy. Papal authority was strengthened. The Bible and tradition were adjudged to be equal sources of truth, and Jerome's Latin Vulgate was to remain as the normative text. On every point, Lutherans, Zwinglians and Calvinists were condemned, along with anything remotely resembling Anabaptism.[2]

Shortly before the Council of Trent was set up, the Pope had approved Ignatius Loyola's 'Society of Jesus'. The Jesuits, as they were more commonly called, would become a dominant force in the Counter-Reformation. The Society of Jesus was in effect a secret society, with secret instructions (*Secreta Monita*), only available to the higher orders in the society. Those who had access to these instructions were to pass them on verbally to trusted members of the lower orders, without it being

Rome's response: the Counter-Reformation

known that any specific written secret instructions existed. The *Secreta Monita* only became public as the result of a military raid on a Jesuit college in Brunswick in the early seventeenth century. The 'instructions' were subsequently translated and printed into many European languages.[3]

With its newly re-affirmed self-confidence and its newly-commissioned Jesuit 'special forces', Rome set out to conquer the rest of the world. Rome began its missions well before any Protestant missions got going. At the forefront of this missionary activity were Spain and Portugal. With their pioneering voyages to Central and South America, the Jesuit missionaries planted Catholicism in the whole of Latin America well before any Protestant missionary activity began.

But there was a little-known darker side to Trent which has subsequently come to light. It was a complex strategy to bring back, by force, the whole of Europe under the heel of Rome. The plan was discussed at the closing stages of the council in the early 1560s. The main outlines of the plan were disclosed by Henry II, king of France, to William, Prince of Orange, on a hunting trip in the Forest of Vincennes, a few miles outside the French capital. What Henry did not know at the time was that William was giving serious consideration to the claims of the gospel, now being proclaimed by Protestant 'heretics' in the United Provinces (similar in geographical extent to modern-day Belgium and the Netherlands) where William's jurisdiction lay. Because William gave no indication of his inner revulsion to the plan, he has gone down in history as 'William the Silent'.[4]

At that time, Spain was the super-power with a correspondingly powerful army and navy and an expanding empire in the 'New World'. She was also solidly Catholic, having all but snuffed out the beginnings of Protestant sympathies in Spain itself. Spain also at that time ruled the United Provinces, and had introduced the Inquisition into those provinces which were beginning to embrace the Reformation. Edict after edict increased the steady toll of those who refused to recant and who

Chapter 13

paid for their fortitude with their own blood. Interestingly, William's knowledge of the plan to subdue his realm and the rest of the United Provinces eventually galvanized him into action. He was a key player in the struggle that would eventually free the Provinces from the yoke of Spanish tyranny. That would not be, however, for more than thirty years.

In outline, the plan to eradicate the Protestant 'heresy' was this:

Firstly, the king of Spain would pick a war with the Protestant French Huguenots, who were dominant in the south of France. The king of France would join in this conflict to stamp out Protestantism from the whole of France. Catholic forces from southern Germany would aim to block the passes into France to prevent any Protestant reinforcements helping the Huguenots.

Secondly, Catholic forces would unite to make war on Germany to root out every last vestige of Luther's heresy.

Thirdly, when this had been achieved, the Duke of Savoy would march on Geneva to destroy the centre of the Protestant heresy.

As England is not mentioned in the plan, it may have been conceived during Mary Tudor's reign (1553–58). Mary appeared at that time to be successfully bringing the English back into the Roman fold.

But 'the best laid schemes', even of evil men, 'gang oft a-gley'.[5] Not long after this hunting trip, the French king, Henry, met his death as the result of a jousting tournament.[6] Parts of the plan were, however, implemented. In 1572, the St Bartholomew's Day massacre in France resulted in tens of thousands of Huguenots being lured into a trap and killed. The Thirty Years' War in central Europe during the early seventeenth century, involving many other European nations, had the estimated effect of halving the population of the continent through war, famine and disease. Eventually, common sense prevailed and a peace treaty was signed in Munster in 1648.

Although not part of the original plan, the Spanish Armada set out in 1588 to subdue 'Protestant' England and bring her back to Rome. In the

Rome's response: the Counter-Reformation

providence of God, largely because of adverse weather and an increasingly effective British navy, the Spanish venture was a complete failure.

A further attempt to overthrow the government of Protestant England was the Gunpowder Plot in 1605, but this was fortunately foiled shortly before it could be put into effect. Even up to the present day, some include in their Bonfire Night celebrations the burning of a 'guy' in memory of the Gunpowder Plot's best remembered conspirator, Guy Fawkes.

It is certain that the Jesuits were involved, behind the scenes, in most if not all of the above plans to suppress the Protestant 'heresy'. By the eighteenth century, because of the disruptive effects of clandestine Jesuit activity, there was mounting pressure for their suppression. Eventually, in 1773, Pope Clement XIV signed a 'Bull' for the Society of Jesus to be suppressed 'for ever'. In signing this document, Clement feared that he was signing his death warrant. Although, at the time, he was in very good health, he died in suspicious circumstances fourteen months later on 22 September 1774.[7]

NOTES

1 The seven sacraments of the Roman Catholic Church are: baptism, the eucharist, confirmation, confession, marriage, holy orders and anointing of the sick (extreme unction).
2 C. P. Hallihan, *The Protestant Reformation* (London: Trinitarian Bible Society, 2017), p. 53.
3 J. A. Wylie, *History of Protestantism*, vol. 2 (London: Cassell and Company, n.d.), p. 411.
4 J. A. Wylie, *History of Protestantism*, vol. 3 (London: Cassell and Company, n.d.), p. 40.
5 Robbie Burns' poem, 'Of Mice and Men'.
6 Wylie, *History*, vol. 3, p. 41.
7 Wylie, *History*, vol. 2, p. 419.

Protestant England and her American colonies

The seventeenth century is probably one of the most controversial periods of church history. And yet it is probably one of the most important. In the sixteenth century, all over Europe the church had undergone a massive upheaval as it struggled to come to terms with the renewing influences of the Bible in the language of the people. Millions had experienced the transforming power of the Holy Spirit in their lives. The European nations would never be the same again. But because millions, too, wanted to hang on to the old order and teachings of the medieval church, the century became a field of conflict.

In England, the death of the Protestant King Edward VI left the nation divided. Henry VIII's staunchly Catholic daughter, Mary, had the strongest claim to the throne. The Protestant party at court, however, following the written instructions of Edward,[1] installed his cousin, 15-year-old Lady Jane Grey, as queen in July 1553; but she only remained as such for nine days. Her claim to the throne was not as out-of-order as might be supposed, but the majority of the nation supported Mary. There was a brief period when England was poised on the brink of civil war, but it was not long before Mary was welcomed into London amid scenes of great jubilation. Queen Jane was deposed, imprisoned in the Tower, and executed some nine months later.

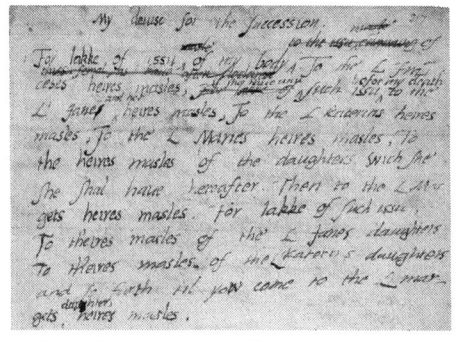

Edward VI's 'Devise for the Succession'

90 A Beginner's Guide to Church History

Thorough-going Protestants knew that Mary's acceptance as queen meant that England would not be a safe place for them. Many fled to the continent to escape the inevitable persecution. Those who stayed, particularly prominent clerics such as Archbishop Cranmer, and Bishops Latimer, Ridley and Hooper, were soon rounded up, imprisoned, and then burnt at the stake for heresy. Altogether nearly three hundred were executed in 'Bloody' Mary's short reign, because they would not renounce their biblically-based faith and revert to Catholicism.

In November 1558 Mary died and her half-sister Elizabeth succeeded her to the throne of England. In many ways, Elizabeth's forty-five-year reign was a golden age of English history. Her first priority on becoming queen was to return England to the Protestant faith. Yet she famously declared that she did not want to 'make windows into men's souls', and was satisfied as long as her subjects gave an outward show of conformity. Elizabeth's influence created a Church of England that, although Protestant, allowed some of the old Catholic traditions to continue.

Elizabeth chose an able set of administrators to aid her during her rule, including William Cecil as Secretary of State and Sir Francis Walsingham in charge of Intelligence. Elizabeth's reign also saw England significantly expand its trade overseas, and in 1580 Sir Francis Drake became the first Englishman to successfully circumnavigate the globe. The arts, too, flourished in England during this period. Shakespeare, Spenser, and Marlowe created poetry and drama, while composers such as Byrd and Tallis worked in Elizabeth's court.

The Puritans

The word Puritan has become very much a 'dirty' word in our times. This agrees with the comment by a senior devil in C. S. Lewis' *Screwtape Letters*, where he says: '..."Puritanism"—and may I remark in passing that the [negative] value we have given to that word is one of the really solid triumphs of the last hundred years?'[2]

Chapter 14

Who then were these men who have become so vilified in recent years? What did they do to earn such a negative reputation? Their nickname, for that is what it was, derived from their desire to live godly lives in accordance with Scripture. This had been what the sincere medieval monks had desired, but because many of them either could not or did not read the Bible, their ideas of godly living were distorted by the teachings of the church.

The Puritans, then, were characterized by careful attention to detail, both in their scholarship and in the practice of their faith. As we saw in chapter 11, John Calvin stands out for his grasp of Scripture truth in the sixteenth century, and the Puritans developed his theology even further, while endeavouring still to remain faithful to Scripture. In Puritan writings we have undoubtedly some of the finest examples of Biblical scholarship coupled with practical application. Many of their works have been published and republished. Some, currently available in paperback form, are still quite readable. Many abridgements and simplified versions have been helpful to English-speaking Christians worldwide.

By and large, the Puritans held to what has been called the 'regulative principle'. Put simply, this means that the whole of our lives as Christians should be governed by the direct teaching or derived principles of the Bible. Many of the exiles who returned from the continent after Mary's death were disappointed at Elizabeth's rather restrictive halfway stance. Nevertheless, during Elizabeth's reign, Puritan ministries began to flourish. One of the early leaders was William Perkins at Cambridge. As more pastors were trained under his influence, the number of Puritan pastors and preachers steadily increased. Some notable students of Perkins were John Robinson (pastor of the group which went on to found the Plymouth Colony), Thomas Goodwin, James Ussher who became Archbishop of Armagh) and Richard Sibbes.

One area in which these men excelled was in spiritual discernment at the pastoral level. Their pithy sayings are also almost legendary.[3]

The King James Bible

As the Bible was at the very heart of the Reformation, it seems fitting that one of the most important events at the beginning of the seventeenth century in England was the publication of the King James Bible, often known as the Authorized Version (AV).

As we saw in chapter 12, William Tyndale's work of translating the Hebrew and Greek texts into common English was the foundation upon which subsequent English versions of the Scriptures were based. Tyndale's martyrdom in 1536 meant that he was unable to complete his work, and this gave rise to several versions of the Bible in English being published. The first of the Stuart kings, James I, although Protestant in his convictions, was uneasy about some of the more radical views of the Puritans. He was also unhappy that there was not just one standard English version of the Bible, so he commissioned the publication of a new version which he would personally authorize and which would also reflect his ecclesiastical views.

In order to achieve this objective, he set up six translation committees comprising both Puritan and High Church scholars, each committee consisting of around eight members. They started work at the end of 1604. They had access to the best available original texts and all previous English translations. Each committee would review and revise all contributions by individual members until a consensus was reached on each passage.

Of all versions of the Bible in English, the Authorized Version, published in 1611, has probably exerted the greatest influence on the English-speaking world.

The Pilgrim Fathers

Another pivotal event which took place early in the seventeenth century was the sailing of the *Mayflower* for America. The hundred or so who ventured on that hazardous undertaking could have had no idea what the outcome of their journey would be. Very much the children of the Reformation, this

Chapter 14

ordinary group of artisans was dissatisfied with the continued restrictions of the state church. At first they emigrated to Holland because, at that time, the Dutch authorities allowed a greater freedom of worship than was permitted in England. After some ten years, the opportunity arose for them to emigrate to one of the newly-formed British colonies on the eastern seaboard of North America. At first they planned to sail on two vessels: the *Mayflower* and the *Speedwell*. After only a few days out at sea from Southampton, the *Speedwell* proved to be unsuitable for an Atlantic crossing and they had to turn back and put into port in Plymouth.

Even though all this had caused a significant delay, they decided to transfer all passengers and essential cargo to the *Mayflower*. It finally sailed from Plymouth on 6 September 1620, some two months later than originally planned. This would mean that they would have to contend with worse weather during the crossing, and that they would not be arriving in the autumn as originally planned, but well into the winter months. Amazingly, despite a very difficult voyage in such cramped conditions, there was no loss of life among the passengers, and one new arrival was welcomed and given the appropriate name of Oceanus!

The Pilgrims had to live on the *Mayflower* for the winter months, rowing ashore to build houses during the day, and returning to the ship at night. Many of them became ill because of the cold and wet. Sadly, about half the people on the *Mayflower* died that first winter from what they described as 'general sickness' of coughs, colds and fevers. Finally, in March 1621, they had built enough houses for everyone to live on land. After a long hard voyage, and an even harder winter, *Mayflower* left the Plymouth Colony to return to England on 5 April 1621.

In the providence of God, a native American Indian turned up that spring who spoke reasonable English. His bi-lingual ability had doubtless been acquired through contact with earlier British settlers. This proved to be a great help for the *Mayflower* group in understanding the best way to obtain food and interact with the Indian population. After a somewhat shaky start, boosted by more immigrants from England over the next two decades, the Plymouth Colony became the dominant group in the foundation and growth of the USA. It is estimated that between 1621 and 1639 some twenty thousand emigrated to New England, mainly to escape Archbishop Laud's restrictive and oppressive policies. There were a significant number among them from the universities.[4]

The English Civil War

This arose out of escalating political, social and religious tensions between King Charles I and Parliament. At Nottingham in August 1642, Charles issued a 'call to arms' against Parliament. The early battles of the ensuing Civil War were inconclusive. The turning point of the war was in 1644 at Marston Moor, when a Parliamentary cavalry officer, Oliver Cromwell, took the initiative. By disciplined and repeated cavalry charges, Cromwell's troopers turned the battle in favour of the Parliamentary forces. After Marston Moor, it was not long before Cromwell's outstanding military skills were recognized and he had become, in effect, the commander-in-chief of the Parliamentary 'New Model Army'. Cromwell's military genius enabled him never to lose a battle, and Parliament to defeat the Royalist forces under King Charles. The king was captured and kept under house arrest for nearly three years. After considerable debate on the Parliamentary side, the decision was eventually made to bring the king to trial. He was found guilty of high treason and executed on 30 January 1649. Charles' death warrant had fifty-nine signatories on it. Opinions have been divided ever since over the justice and wisdom of this act of regicide. Charles Spencer, himself a descendant of Charles I, in his

Chapter 14

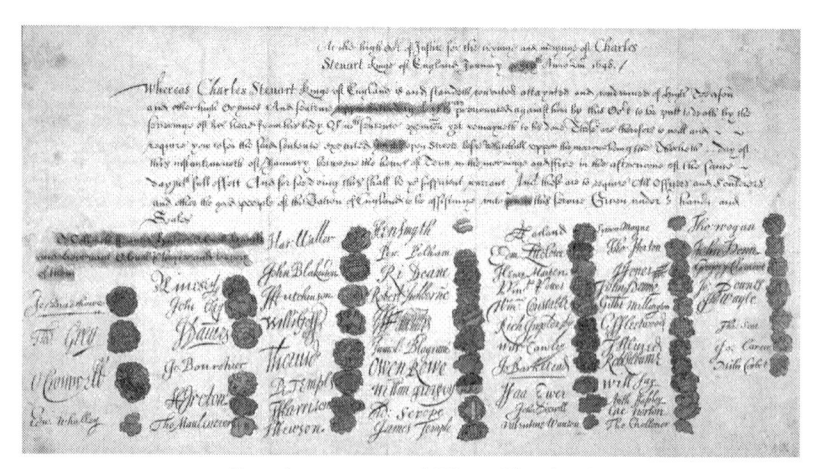

Death warrant of King Charles I

book, *Killers of the King*, comes to the following surprising conclusion: 'It is striking how many fascinating and notable figures colluded to end [Charles'] life. They deserve, in my view, to be remembered with respect for their sacrifices.'[5]

Another contentious aspect of the Civil War is Cromwell's Irish campaign, particularly the battles at Drogheda and Wexford. The generally-accepted view has been, until recently, that Cromwell's forces massacred the Irish Catholic inhabitants of both towns. The Irish writer, Tom Reilly (born in Drogheda), in his book, *Cromwell, an Honourable Enemy*, comes to a somewhat different conclusion. Reilly maintains that the Irish campaign was a hard-fought one between the Royalist garrisons only and the Parliamentary army. Reilly also shows that there is strong documentary evidence that, in Ireland, Cromwell held rigidly to the Parliamentary 'rules of engagement', one of which was that only those bearing arms were to be attacked.[6] Some civilians were inevitably killed during the Irish campaign, mainly because of being caught in the crossfire or the general confusion of war.

Protestant England and her American colonies

NOTES

1. A picture of Edward's 'Devise for the Succession' can be found online at https://en.wikipedia.org/wiki/Edward_VI_of_England#Devise_for_the_succession. (Accessed 5th March 2019.)
2. C. S. Lewis, *Screwtape Letters*, letter 10 (Glasgow: William Collins, 1977), p. 55.
3. See I. D. E. Thomas, *A Puritan Golden Treasury* (Edinburgh: Banner of Truth Trust, 1977).
4. John Brown, *The English Puritans* (Fearn: Christian Focus Publications, 1998), p. 127.
5. Charles Spencer, *Killers of the King* (London: Bloomsbury Publishing, 2014), p. 321.
6. Tom Reilly, *Cromwell, an Honourable Enemy* (Dingle: Mount Eagle Publications Ltd., 1999).

From 'Christian' republic to constitutional monarchy

In sixteenth century Scotland, the Reformation, mainly under the influence of John Knox, had been more thorough than in England, particularly in the realm of church government. Each congregation was now ruled by elders, who met regularly with elders of neighbouring churches. There was also a General Assembly of the whole church once a year, but no permanent hierarchy. The medieval hierarchy including bishops and archbishops had been abolished.

Between 1629 and 1640, Charles I had ruled Britain for eleven years without a parliament. The king and his archbishop (William Laud) aimed to bring the government of the church in Scotland into line with that of the English church. By means of the Court of High Commission, which operated outside Parliamentary jurisdiction, the king gave Laud the authority to impose the Church of England prayer book on the Scottish churches. Scotland rose in revolt and vast numbers signed the 'National Covenant' upholding the Presbyterian form of government. The signing began in Greyfriars churchyard, Edinburgh, on 28 February 1638. Events soon escalated and war broke out between Scotland and the English crown.

In order to finance this war, in 1640 Charles summoned Parliament. What Charles had not realized was that there was now a sizeable Puritan party in Parliament who supported the Scots. If the king's war was to be approved, then some of the recent legislation affecting the church would need to be amended or repealed. The result was a stand-off between the king and Parliament. In 1642, Charles took up arms against Parliament and, in effect, left the business of running the country in the hands of those MPs who had been recently elected. This Parliament, called the Long

From 'Christian' republic to constitutional monarchy

Parliament, sat throughout the Civil War and was not finally dissolved until March 1653. This was the first time that the English Parliament had ever governed independently from the monarch.

The Westminster Assembly

Soon after the beginning of the English Civil War, Parliament called together a committee of over one hundred clergymen from all over England to advise them on 'the good government of the Church'.[1] This body, the Westminster Assembly of Divines, convened on 1 July 1643, and continued daily meetings for more than five years. The majority were Presbyterians, along with a sizeable group of Erastians and a few Independents. There were also twelve Scottish commissioners. The Presbyterians were in favour of the Church of England following the Scottish Presbyterian model, the Erastians considered that the church should be under state control, while the Independents wanted the church to be completely free from state interference.

The Westminster Assembly

Chapter 15

After several months of debate, no agreement was reached on the subject of church government, so Parliament instructed them to draw up a Confession of Faith covering all other points of doctrine. The end result was what is now called the Westminster Confession. Other associated documents were the *Directory of Public Worship*, which replaced the *Book of Common Prayer*, and the Westminster Larger and Shorter Catechisms. A strong Presbyterian influence pervades these 'Westminster Standards'. This is partly explained by the fact that in 1643 Parliament signed the Scottish 'Solemn League and Covenant',[2] because Scotland's help was needed in the Civil War against the Royalists.

The Westminster Assembly and the Confession it produced have been described as 'the high-water mark of the Reformation'. Richard Baxter, the minister at Kidderminster, although not part of the Assembly, said that 'the Christian world had never seen a synod of more excellent Divines'.[3]

While the Assembly was agreeing its confessional documents, pamphlets were being produced by others outside Parliament urging greater freedom of the press and of religion. Such dissent was supported by the army, and that support became all the more significant because its leaders (Thomas Fairfax and Oliver Cromwell) had become the real power in England after their defeat of Royalist forces. Late in 1648 the army leaders feared that Parliament would reach a compromise with the defeated king that would destroy the gains they had made for Puritanism. In December 1648, the army purged Parliament of members considered unsatisfactory and in January 1649 King Charles was tried and executed. These remaining MPs have sometimes been referred to as the 'Rump Parliament'.

The Commonwealth and Protectorate

In May 1649, the Rump Parliament formally abolished the monarchy and the House of Lords, and declared Britain to be a Commonwealth (or Republic). During the following eleven years, various attempts were made to reconstruct some form of workable parliamentary system, but none

From 'Christian' republic to constitutional monarchy

proved to be successful. It is not surprising that those skilled at winning battles were not necessarily going to be competent at civil government. In addition, the abolition of the monarchy was too much of a seismic shift for the general populace to stomach. Another reason for the failure to produce a workable form of government was the unrealistic aim of achieving a truly Christian society.

The most productive period of the Commonwealth was probably the Protectorate,[4] where Cromwell's desire for freedom of worship was put into effect. An example of this was in December 1655. In response to approaches from the Jewish leader Menasseh ben Israel of Amsterdam, the 'Whitehall Conference' was set up to allow the Jews freedom to settle in England. In the two weeks of discussions, no explicit decision was reached to frame any Act of Parliament. However, two of the judges in attendance, John Glynne and William Steele, offered their learned opinion that there was no existing law on the books against the Jews coming in, because their original expulsion had been by royal decree and not by Parliamentary vote. As a result, the conference had the effect of lowering the barrier that had been keeping Jews from settling in the country. The Republican Parliament also gave American Indians British citizenship.

Even though the Puritans in Parliament were unable to set up a lasting workable system of government, Puritan pastors and preachers flourished during this period. In particular, those of Independent (Congregational or Baptist) persuasion significantly increased in number.

The restoration of the monarchy

In 1658 Oliver Cromwell, the Lord Protector, died of natural causes. His son Richard was asked to succeed him, but was neither willing nor able to continue in the role his father had filled. Concerned that the country would drift into chaos, General Monck, who had fought for both sides in the Civil War, met with other prominent national figures to consider the way forward. They decided to ask Charles II to take the throne of

Chapter 15

England, Scotland and Ireland. Charles readily agreed and was received in London in May 1660. There could not be a greater contrast between the two leaders, Oliver Cromwell and King Charles II. Cromwell was a man of strict moral honesty and integrity, a typical Puritan. Cromwell was also a well-loved family man who, as his many letters show, took a keen pastoral interest in his family's spiritual welfare. Charles was the exact opposite, an unprincipled, untrustworthy 'playboy'. His mistresses ran into double figures, and he was at times loath to tear himself away from his bedchamber to see to government business. He often broke his promises, some of which he clearly never had any intention of keeping. Such was the 'Merry Monarch'.

One keynote at the beginning of Charles' regime was to obtain revenge over those who had had anything to do with his father's execution. Those involved in his father's death were promised pardon, although many saw through the hollowness of this 'promise'. Once Charles was firmly in power, the regicides and some of their associates were mercilessly hunted down. Those unable to escape were hung, drawn and quartered. Some remained on the run abroad until they died.[5] The Restoration Parliament also indiscriminately swept aside all the legislation of the Commonwealth period, setting the clock back to the 1630s. Even blood sports such as bear-baiting and cock-fighting, which had been banned during the Commonwealth period, were now permitted.

The Act of Uniformity

In 1662, the notorious Act of Uniformity was passed, enforcing by law the use of the 1662 Prayer Book. The Act had been deliberately designed to oust Puritan pastors from the Church of England. It had the desired effect, as nearly two thousand voluntarily resigned their positions, refusing to conform. They were the first significant group of non-militant nonconformists. Most were Congregationalists, but some were Presbyterian or Baptist. At a stroke they lost their homes and their incomes. Many lost their congregations. Because of other restrictive acts which followed (the Conventicle Act and the Five Mile Act), those preachers who refused to be muzzled were often imprisoned. One of the best known of these is John Bunyan, who wrote his *Pilgrim's Progress* while in Bedford Jail. Baptists in the West Country came up with a novel approach to these restrictions. Newhouse Baptist Church was built at the intersection of the three counties of Devon, Dorset and Somerset. There was a door behind the pulpit so that if the authorities were approaching from one county, the preacher could be given the tip-off to escape into one of the others.

The Glorious Revolution

In 1685 Charles died and was succeeded by his brother James, an avowed Catholic (Charles had no legitimate offspring). It was not long before James' actions began to alarm leading Protestants. He quickly filled leading government posts with Catholics and created a predominantly Catholic army. Displaced Protestants were summarily dismissed without compensation. The final straw came when it was announced that the Queen had finally produced a male heir to the throne. Seven eminent Englishmen, including one bishop and six prominent politicians of both Whig and Tory persuasions[6] wrote to William of Orange, James' nephew and son-in-law. They invited him to come over from Holland with an army to redress the nation's grievances and take the throne. They assured him that he would be accepted by the majority in the nation. William agreed and assembled a Protestant army, numbering some 21,000, drawn from several European countries. He set sail on 1 November 1688, with a very large fleet of five hundred ships. Initially William's invading army was held in port by a westerly wind. However, the wind soon changed to an easterly direction, favourable to the invading fleet, but keeping James' English fleet in port. The easterly wind persisted sufficiently for William and his army to land at Brixham in Devon. In the meantime, James had

Chapter 15

assembled an army at Salisbury. The total number of James' armed forces outnumbered William's by two to one, but many were stationed in other parts of the country. As William's army began its slow progress towards London, James fled to the continent.

On arriving in London, William was asked to carry on the government and summon a Parliament. When this 'Convention' Parliament met (22 January, 1689), it agreed, after some debate, to treat James's flight as an abdication and to offer the crown jointly to William and his wife Mary, with an accompanying Declaration of Rights. The Convention then turned itself into a proper Parliament and large parts of the Declaration into a 'Bill of Rights'. The main features of this bill were:

- It provided for a Protestant succession to the throne of England and barred Roman Catholics from the throne.
- It abolished the Crown's power to suspend laws.
- It declared a standing army illegal in time of peace without the consent of Parliament.
- It firmly established the principles of frequent Parliaments, free elections and freedom of speech within Parliament.
- It allowed freedom of worship to all except Roman Catholics, who were only allowed to practise their religion privately.

The United States' 'Bill of Rights' was modelled on the English 'Bill of Rights'.

This settlement, often called the 'Glorious Revolution', marked a considerable triumph for Whig views. It permanently established Parliament as the ruling power of England. Some modern historians have objected to calling the events of 1688/9 'The Glorious Revolution'[7] and have considered that it should be regarded as a foreign invasion akin to the Norman Conquest of 1066. Democratically, it was a huge step forward and therefore warrants the name 'glorious'. In England the revolution was bloodless; but, in a sense, the real revolution had taken place during the momentous days of the civil war.

From 'Christian' republic to constitutional monarchy

James soon regained his composure and in early 1689 landed in Dublin, aiming to rally support from the Irish Catholics. This provoked a Catholic/Protestant conflict, with other European nations becoming involved. At the decisive 'Battle of the Boyne' in July 1690, William and those allied to him overcame James' opposition and James again fled to the continent.

NOTES

1. From the *Grand Remonstrance*, 1 December 1641.
2. The Solemn League and Covenant (1643) was an agreement between the English and Scots by which the Scots agreed to support the English Parliamentarians in their disputes with the Royalists. Both countries pledged to work for a civil and religious union of England, Scotland and Ireland under Presbyterian church government.
3. Mark Chapman, *Anglicanism: a very short introduction* (Oxford: Oxford University Press 2006), p.51.
4. The title 'Lord Protector' was given to Oliver Cromwell when he agreed to act as 'Head of State' and 'Head of Government' of the Republic, a position he held from 1653 to 1658.
5. Charles Spencer, *Killers of the King*, chapters 5–15.
6. The seventeenth-century Whigs in Parliament were radicals, political successors of the earlier Puritans. The seventeenth-century Tories generally had royalist sympathies.
7. Lucy Worseley, BBC series 'Britain's biggest Fibs', 2017.

The First Great Awakening

The decline of Puritanism

As the seventeenth century drew to its close, it appeared that, in the English-speaking world, freedom had now been assured to all Bible-believing Christians to worship God according to their consciences. In essence, the Puritan movement of the past 140 years had made great changes to the religious life of the nation. But it was not long before there was evidence of serious moral and spiritual decline. False teachings and sceptical notions were being heard from church pulpits, and public morality was deteriorating. Gin drinking, immoral plays, prostitution, and blood sports were all on the increase. Increase in crime meant that public hangings were more frequent and were becoming increasingly popular family viewing. There was no doubt about it: in the early 1700s Britain was in a state of serious spiritual and moral decline.

The question has often been asked: 'How could a nation with such spiritual giants as the late seventeenth-century Puritans, slide so quickly into such moral depravity?' Doubtless there were several factors, but one in particular is related to what had occurred a generation earlier. I refer to the 1662 Act of Uniformity, which resulted in nearly two thousand pastors being displaced from their congregations and then being persecuted for the following twenty-five years. Not only pastors were affected by the Act. Academics in the universities were displaced if they refused to conform. Suddenly, the previously strong Puritan influence was removed from those being trained for the Christian ministry. The supply of 'new blood' to provide Bible-believing preachers suddenly dried up. If their opponents had but realized it, this legislation was a master-stroke in dampening down Puritan and evangelical influence in Britain.

But there were notable exceptions to the spiritual decline. The hymn-writer Isaac Watts lived during these times, as did the Bible commentator Matthew Henry and the nonconformist leader Philip Doddridge.

The divine response

God was not taken by surprise at what was happening; he never is. Even as the spiritual and moral gloom deepened, he was bringing into the world his men for those times. The first of these was John Wesley, who was born in 1703 into a growing family in the rectory at Epworth, Lincolnshire. As a very young child John was rescued from an attic window as the thatched-roof house below was ablaze. He would later refer to himself as 'a brand plucked from the burning'. As John was growing up, joined by his brother Charles in 1707, Matthew Henry was coming to the end of writing his classic, *A Method for Prayer*. He completed the book in 1712, just before moving from his twenty-five-year pastorate in Chester to take up a similar position in London. In the late summer of 1712, Matthew Henry also preached a series of sermons which were aimed at encouraging Christians to develop regular daily times of prayer. We do not know how many heard these sermons, or how much they took note of Henry's exhortations or his book. What we do know is that within a very few years of 1712, God had brought into the world those who would bring about a great change. Some of the greatest men of the eighteenth century were born immediately after Matthew Henry preached his sermons in London. Daniel Rowland, who would become a leader among the Welsh Calvinistic Methodists, was born in 1713. George Whitefield, who spearheaded the awakening in England in the late 1730s, was born in 1714. Howell Harris, another leading Welsh Calvinistic Methodist, was born the same year. Several other lesser-known eighteenth-century Christian leaders were also born around that time, such as James Hervey, William Romaine, Walker of Truro and John Berridge. As God works through his people's prayers, it is not unreasonable to make the connection. It was Matthew Henry

Chapter 16

himself who said, 'When God intends great mercy for his people, the first thing he does is to set them a-praying.'

The spiritual state of affairs was somewhat better in the North American colonies. The foundations of their society were largely free from the unhelpful baggage that had hindered spiritual progress in Britain. They had not experienced a brutal and costly civil war. The government of the churches had been much freer from the outset, underpinned by the 'Mayflower Compact'.[1] A good number of competent and biblically-sound pastors were over the churches, and an influential training college for pastors, known as the Log College,[2] was set up in 1727. But spiritual decline had set in here as well as in England and several leaders in the churches were concerned about the trends.

The Holy Club

The 'Holy Club' was one of the nicknames given to a society at Oxford University, which was started in 1728, with Charles Wesley as one of its founder members. The club's members practised early rising, lengthy devotions, and self-discipline, aiming to leave not a moment of time wasted. These practices gave rise to the name 'Methodist', which has survived to this day. They were devoted to the Church of England, and also engaged in good works, visiting Oxford's prisons and Poor House. They helped financially where they could and paid for a school for prisoners' children. They met regularly for Bible study using the Greek New Testament, and also studied the writings of learned men. In 1729, John Wesley returned to Oxford University and with his leadership qualities he soon took charge of the club's activities. In 1732 George Whitefield entered Pembroke College at Oxford, and was introduced to the Holy Club during the following year. By that time the society's membership had grown to double figures, with a similar number of associates. Despite their high ideals and intentions, these early Methodists were not evangelical. Their religion was works-based and as a result gave them no spiritual satisfaction.

The First Great Awakening

George Whitefield

It was with Whitefield that spiritual change would begin. He had begun to read Henry Scougal's little book, *The Life of God in the Soul of Man*, and through it came under deep conviction of sin. In the spring of 1735, after months of spiritual struggle, as he puts it in his own words: 'God was pleased to remove my heavy load, to enable me to lay hold of His dear Son by a living faith, and by giving me the Spirit of adoption, to seal me even to the day of everlasting redemption.'[3]

In later life when visiting Oxford he would visit the very spot where God had given him the new birth. It was a life-changing experience for Whitefield. He was ordained the following year by the Bishop of Gloucester and preached his first sermon in Gloucester a week later. That first sermon, which was purported to have 'driven fifteen people mad', marked the beginning of his life's work. Initially during 1736 and 1737, Whitefield preached wherever he was invited, mainly in the south of England—Gloucester, Bristol and London, plus many other smaller towns and villages. And it was preaching which not only startled the nation, but which over the next thirty-five years brought about huge changes in the spiritual state of Britain and the American colonies.

Stirrings in Massachusetts

The first sign of any change on the American Continent came in late 1734 in Northampton, Massachusetts. As Jonathan Edwards, the pastor of the Congregational Church in Northampton, puts it: 'It was in the latter part of December [1734] that the Spirit of God began extraordinarily to set in, and wonderfully to work among us; and very suddenly, one

A Beginner's Guide to Church History **109**

Chapter 16

after another, five or six persons were to all appearances savingly converted...'[4]

Shortly after these events in Massachusetts, John Wesley arrived in America, having responded to a call for missionaries to the newly-founded colony of Georgia. It was during the sea voyage to America that Wesley met the Moravians.[5] In observing their lifestyle and in conversation with them, Wesley began to realize that, though deeply religious himself, he was an unconverted man. Partly because of this, his stay in Georgia was beset with problems. His strong personality brought him into conflict with others in the church, and he decided to return to England in late 1737. In early 1738 his search for true salvation became more intense and was not relieved until May, and the famous Aldersgate Street meeting, where he said that his 'heart was strangely warmed'. It was a whole new beginning for John Wesley and the start of an even longer ministry than George Whitefield's.

When John Wesley was in America, he had written twice to the Holy Club in Oxford requesting extra help. After lengthy consideration of Wesley's appeal, Whitefield decided to go to Georgia, but due to various delays did not set sail until early 1738. He was not aware of Wesley's premature return, and their ships must have passed near the coast of England. Unlike the unconverted Wesley, Whitefield was well received in the newly-established colony. Although its inhabitants probably only numbered in their hundreds, many came to hear him preach. It was while on this first trip that the concept of an orphanage began to take shape in his thinking. He arrived back in England in late 1738, not only to find that both the Wesley brothers had been converted, but that there was evidence of lasting fruit from his earlier preaching in England. On his return, Whitefield resumed his preaching ministry, particularly now to very large congregations in the open air.[6] John Wesley, on the other hand, was initially reluctant to do such work, but with Whitefield's encouragement, soon began to preach with confidence, particularly in

The First Great Awakening

the Bristol area. In August 1739 Whitefield left the work in England in the hands of John Wesley and returned to Georgia to supervise the beginning of the construction of the orphanage in Savannah. He interspersed his time in Savannah with three preaching tours to the other American colonies. It is estimated that, during that visit, over half the population of the thirteen colonies heard him preach, with significant and lasting effect. During this visit, friendships were also forged with many of the American Christian leaders, including Jonathan Edwards in Northampton and the Tennent family near Philadelphia.

Opposition and division

Wherever there is spiritual blessing, opposition follows hard on its heels. Right from the start of his ministry, Whitefield had his critics. Many outside the church were dismissive and called the Methodists 'Enthusiasts'. There was opposition from within the Church of England, too, and before long many church doors were closed to Whitefield, the Wesleys and their associates. The preachers responded by adopting 'field-preaching' with beneficial results.

More distressing were the divisions which began to appear among the leaders of the revival. The Wesleys came from an anti-Calvinistic background, which affected their theological stance throughout their lives. Whitefield, on the other hand, was a Calvinist, very much a child of the Puritans. At first Whitefield advised that they should avoid preaching on the controversial subject of predestination, but within weeks John Wesley had preached a sermon against it and had had it published. An open breach between Whitefield and the Wesleys occurred in 1741 and they came to an agreement to work separately. Because the harvest-field was so large, it was possible for them not to transgress on each other's territory. Later, Whitefield attempted a formal reconciliation between the Calvinistic Methodists, the Wesleyan Methodists and the Moravians, but it came to nothing. The separation doubtless acted as a spur to Whitefield who, although he still preached in England, spent most of his efforts in America, Wales, Scotland and Ireland. He crossed the Atlantic thirteen times and paid fifteen visits to Scotland and two to Ireland, as well as preaching in every county in England. After having preached a total of around 18,000 times, George Whitefield died in 1770 at the age of fifty-six during his seventh visit to America. He is buried in Newburyport, Massachusetts.

The Wesleys, on the other hand, concentrated their efforts on establishing the work in England, particularly the care of converts, who attended special classes organized for them.[7] Neither the Wesleys or Whitefield ever formally separated from the Church of England, but the Wesleyan Methodist Church was officially inaugurated a few years after John Wesley's death in 1788.

Whitefield's evangelistic methods

To those who were awakened by his preaching, George Whitefield based his approach on practices similar to those of the Puritans. These were:

- He made a powerful application of the gospel in his sermons, often with stern warnings to those who might refuse the offer of salvation in Christ.
- He made no appeal for people to make public profession of salvation, not wishing to meddle in what he regarded as the Holy Spirit's domain.
- He made himself available for those who wanted to speak to him about their spiritual state, but always urged them to go directly to the Lord.
- He never gave seekers reason to believe that speaking with him had any efficacy, emphasizing that salvation is a divine work, between the soul and God alone.
- He refused to count converts, believing that only the Judgement Day would reveal who the real converts were.

The First Great Awakening

Effects of the eighteenth-century awakening

Numerous agencies promoting Christian work arose as a result of the eighteenth-century revival. Anti-slavery societies, prison reform groups and relief agencies for the poor were started. Numerous missionary societies were also formed. The Religious Tract Society was organized, and the British and Foreign Bible Society was established. Hospitals and schools multiplied. In particular, John Wesley encouraged Christians to become active in social reform. He himself spoke out strongly against the slave trade and encouraged William Wilberforce in his anti-slavery crusade.

NOTES

1. The 'Mayflower Compact' was an agreement signed by all the male passengers on the *Mayflower* to set up as free and equitable a society as possible. It included a clause expressing a desire to live at peace with the native American Indians.
2. S. M. Houghton, *Sketches from Church History* (Edinburgh: Banner of Truth Trust, 1980), p. 182.
3. Arnold Dallimore, *George Whitefield*, vol. 1 (London: Banner of Truth Trust, 1970), p. 77.
4. Houghton, *Sketches*, p. 183.
5. The Moravians seem to trace their roots back to the followers of John Huss. In the eighteenth century they were very active in missionary work in northern Europe and beyond.
6. Where Whitefield preached in very large public open spaces, his congregations could often be counted in tens of thousands.
7. The Methodist class meetings consisted of around 12 people and typically met for 1–1½ hours, during which time each person would have an opportunity to share their experience of deepening love in Christ.

The gospel goes global

In 1747 the American theologian Jonathan Edwards published a book with an extremely long title. Its opening words were *An Humble Attempt...*[1] and it has since been generally known by this designation. So what was the significance of Edwards' publication in relation to the history of the Church?

In his *Humble Attempt*, Edwards strongly urges Christians to pray regularly for revival. He bases his exhortation on Zechariah 8:20–22, and encourages Christians (particularly pastors) to set aside regular days for prayer for 'special seasons of mercy'. Edwards envisages corporate prayer, but recommends that if there were others who could not meet physically for prayer, then they could set aside a time for private intercession on the designated day. This concept of what Edwards called 'a concert of prayer', was not original to him. The Scottish evangelical pastor John Erskine had organized a 'concert of prayer' throughout Scotland in 1744. So what was the effect of Edwards' challenge? The sales of the *Humble Attempt*, compared with some of his other books, were disappointing.

But in 1784, an English Particular Baptist pastor named John Sutcliff received a box of books from a pastor friend in Scotland. Included among the books was a copy of *An Humble Attempt*. After reading the book, Sutcliff began to circulate it among his fellow Baptist pastors. Inspired by Edwards, Sutcliff and his friends issued a call for the pastors of the Northamptonshire Baptist Association to set apart the first Monday evening of every month for prayer for the heathen and the coming kingdom of Christ. One of the younger pastors in this group was none other than William Carey, who regularly attended these special prayer meetings. It had already been Carey's burden that the 'heathen' should hear the gospel, and during these meetings his conviction deepened. Another book by Jonathan Edwards which had a profound effect on Carey was *The Life and Diary of David Brainerd*. (Brainerd had pioneered missionary work among the North American Indians.) In October 1792, Carey persuaded his fellow pastors to set up 'The Particular Baptist Association for the Propagation of the Gospel among the Heathen'.

Plans were soon set in hand for the Association to send out their first missionaries. But whom would they send and where would they go? Carey himself would be the answer to the first question, and the answer to the second came by a letter to Carey from John Thomas. Thomas was a surgeon who had just returned from Bengal and was seeking more personnel to establish a Christian mission in Calcutta. Carey and Thomas would be the first two to be sent out by the Association. There were, however, a number of obstacles. The East India Company, Britain's trading arm in India, was unlikely to license them, particularly with France now being at war with Britain. Also, Carey's wife Dorothy was very hesitant about the family embarking on such a hazardous undertaking. In the end, after several twists and turns of providence, the first missionary party of eight people set sail from Dover on 13 June 1793 on the Danish East Indiaman, the *Kron Princessa Maria*. Because of the war with France, even though it was a Danish ship, they had a British frigate as a naval escort as far as the Bay of Biscay.

William Carey

Chapter 17

During the five-month voyage, Carey began to learn Bengali from Thomas, who was attempting the translation of the book of Genesis. The captain of the ship showed great kindness to the missionary group. Carey described him as 'one of the most polite, accomplished gentlemen that ever bore the name of sea-captain'.[2] Among other things, he allowed them to conduct services on Sundays, to which the other passengers were invited. Dorothy Carey and her sister Kitty were not good sailors, but after rounding the southernmost tip of Africa (the Cape of Good Hope), Dorothy set her mind more on arriving in India than going back to England. Shortly after rounding the Cape, they also ran into a violent storm which caused considerable damage to the masts and rigging. Carey and Thomas helped with the repairs, which took eleven days to complete.

India at last!

On reaching the mouth of the River Ganges, as the missionaries had no permits to land in India, they transferred to a smaller local fishing vessel, which took them the sixteen miles into Calcutta itself without attracting any interest from officials.[3] When their small craft stopped on the way at a market town, Thomas took the opportunity of preaching to crowds of locals, who listened to his discourse for three hours. Afterwards they were invited to supper, and were asked to return. Truly, they 'hit the ground running'. They first set foot on Indian soil in Calcutta, in effect as 'illegal immigrants', on 11 November 1793. Finally at their destination, a city of some 200,000, Carey describes his feelings as being akin to Paul's on his visit to the pagan city of Athens.[4]

There were many obstacles which the small group of Christian believers faced as they began their new life on the Indian sub-continent. They had very little money and needed somewhere to live. Thomas' wife was already there, but she was dismayed when eight of them turned up on the doorstep, not just the two men. Somehow, for the next eight months they managed to eke out an existence in various temporary rented accommodation, and survived largely due to the help and kindness of sympathetic Europeans. When, therefore, in the late summer of 1794, Carey and Thomas were given the offer of running an indigo manufacturing facility at Mudnabatty, 250 miles north of Calcutta, they regarded it as God's provision for them. Their combined income would be £500 p.a., which was ample to support them all. No sooner had they moved than great sorrow struck the Carey household, when their five-year-old son, Peter, contracted a fever and died. Dorothy never recovered from Peter's death. Carey found this deeply distressing and wrote at the time, 'My poor wife must be considered as insane, and is the occasion of great sorrow.'[5] Dorothy remained in need of care right up to her death in 1807.

Despite all his problems and difficulties, the five years spent at Mudnabatty were foundational to Carey's future work. He was a tent-maker missionary. As well as running the indigo production, he had a full schedule of language study, translating and preaching. His Sunday congregations would sometimes number several hundred. He started a fledgling school, and all the while he endeavoured to cultivate the friendship of the locals, without compromising his Christian witness. But in all these labours, there was as yet not a single Indian convert.

In 1799, the indigo facility was devastated by the monsoon floods, and Carey decided to start up his own facility a few miles away with the help of his 16-year-old son Felix. They had hardly set themselves up when reinforcements arrived from England, including the Marshman family and the printer, William Ward. They would turn out to be a huge help in establishing the mission, but faced the same problem that Carey had on his arrival—they were not licensed by the East India Company, so could not live on British territory. The Danes again came to their assistance and offered them all a site at Serampore. The buildings already on the site, with suitable alterations, were ideal for establishing a missionary community and became their permanent base.

Chapter 17

Mission established

It was at Serampore that the work of Carey and his colleagues bore most fruit. Although their primary purpose was preaching the gospel, the missionaries became involved in relief of the poor in and around the town, and promoting education and social reforms. It was partly through the efforts of Carey and his colleagues that the practice of burning widows (*sati*) was legally proscribed.[6] They established more than a hundred 'monitorial' schools[7] in the region. Hannah Marshman established the first girls' school at Serampore, which received much public approval. Carey made an outstanding contribution to Indian literature through the Serampore Mission Press, founded in 1800. Carey and his two associates also established the Serampore College in 1818, which was also the first college in Asia to award degrees.

Soon after they set up at Serampore, the first Hindu, Krishna Pal, was converted and baptized. One of his hymns, translated into English, is still to be found in some hymn books.[8] Despite this slow start, by 1821 more than 1400 converts had been baptized, over half of them native Indians.[9] One of the most serious setbacks Carey experienced was a fire in his printing workshop in 1812, which destroyed many valuable Bible manuscripts being prepared for publication in Indian languages. Despite this disaster, in Carey's lifetime he and Marshman supervised the translation and printing of the whole or part of the Bible into more than forty Indian languages and dialects. His work in translating Indian literature into English has also been recognized as having had a beneficial influence on education in the Indian sub-continent.

Carey's herculean labours in India certainly warrant him being given the title, 'Father of Modern Missions'. But many others were to follow hard on his heels. In 1812, Princeton Seminary was founded in New Jersey, USA. Right from its inception, the seminary had a missionary outlook. Monthly 'Concert of Prayer' meetings were held, and the result was a steady stream of graduates going abroad as missionaries. In its first fifty years, 127 graduates went abroad, among other places to Turkey, Afghanistan, West Africa, northern China, and Brazil. They preached the gospel, translated the Scriptures, educated the young, published books and trained up local pastors.

The late eighteenth and early nineteenth centuries saw the establishment of several other denominational missionary societies: the London Missionary Society (Congregational) in 1795, the Church Missionary Society (Anglican) in 1799, and the American Baptist Mission Board in 1814.

This combined missionary impetus in the early nineteenth century was the most significant advance of the Christian gospel since the days of the apostles. The gospel was being proclaimed among the nations. The majority of these early pioneers were of a Calvinistic persuasion.

NOTES

1. The full title of Edwards' treatise is: *An humble attempt to promote explicit agreement and visible union of God's people in extraordinary prayer for the revival of religion and the advancement of Christ's Kingdom on earth, pursuant to Scripture-promises and prophecies concerning the last time.*
2. Timothy George, *Faithful Witness* (Leicester: IVP, 1992), p. 88.
3. Before the British Empire was established, the British East India Company controlled British interests on the Indian sub-continent. British nationals were not allowed to live on 'British' territory without a licence.
4. Acts 17:16.
5. George, *Faithful Witness*, p. 109.
6. George, *Faithful Witness*, p. 152.
7. The monitorial school method was based on the abler pupils being used as 'helpers' to the teacher, passing on the information they had learned to other students.
8. 'O thou, my soul, forget no more the Friend who all thy misery bore.'
9. As well as making a credible profession of faith, all converted Hindus were required to renounce the evils of the caste system.

Revivals and revivalism

As we saw in chapter 16, during the 1730s and 1740s the churches in the American colonies experienced a great spiritual awakening, often referred to as the First Great Awakening. Partly as a result of that spiritual awakening, the American theologian Jonathan Edwards encouraged ministers on both sides of the Atlantic to pray specifically for revival, because it was the chief means by which the kingdom of Christ was expanded and maintained. Edwards' definition of revival was that it was a time when God sovereignly granted to his church a much greater measure of those operations of the Holy Spirit which were always present among the people of God.

In 1756, during those revival times, a Christian college was established at Princeton, New Jersey, which became one of the most significant influences upon the growing emergent nation of America. In its first eighty years it produced two thousand five hundred graduates, many of whom were men of Christian conviction and filled places of influence in American society. But perhaps more significant were the five hundred of them who entered the Christian ministry and, thanks in part to the continued practical godliness of Princeton presidents, became preachers having similar convictions about revival to Edwards and his contemporaries.

This period of American history up to about 1830 was noted for a series of further revivals which affected all denominations: Presbyterians, Congregationalists, Baptists, Methodists and Anglicans. It was not a period of continuous revival but, rather, punctuated with awakenings every few years. These awakenings were not without their effect on the population expansion westwards through Pennsylvania into the Mississippi valley. It was true religious experience which prepared those early pioneers for the hardships and heroism which the advance westwards would require.

Revivals and revivalism

These men and the people they served lived plain and resolute lives amid astonishing hardships. There were no mills to grind flour for bread and no roads bringing goods across the mountains ... log cabins—made without saws, planes or nails—provided the only homes ... Worse than these deprivations was the peril of attacks from Indians.[1]

During this period of revivals there was a Second Great Awakening[2] which lasted from the late 1790s well into the nineteenth century. Some of the churches, particularly in the frontier areas, saw tremendous increases in membership over many years. 'In the first decade of the nineteenth century the Methodist Episcopal Church saw an increase of 167.8% while, in the same period, the population of the United States increased by only 34.6%.'[3]

Apart from special seasons of prayer and fasting, no special methods, techniques or even campaigns were used to promote the revivals. Even more surprising was the fact that none of the preachers were what one might call outstanding, but all were used in the revivals.

A considerable body of men, for a long period before the Second Great Awakening, preached the same message as they did during the revival but with vastly different consequences ... Nothing was clearer to those who saw the events than that God was sovereignly pleased to bless human instrumentality in such a way that the success could be attributed to him alone.[4]

Misplaced optimism

At the beginning of the nineteenth century, a mood of optimism pervaded the evangelical churches in America. They had experienced an extended time of revivals which had brought many into the kingdom of God. The missionary movement had mushroomed and every year more and more missionaries were going out to evangelize the rest of the world. Many

Chapter 18

thought that the church of Christ was on the cusp of establishing the kingdom of Christ worldwide, which would usher in a millennial 'golden age' when 'the earth will be filled with the knowledge of the glory of the LORD as the waters cover the sea'.[5]

As we know from our vantage point two hundred years on, things did not work out as many had hoped. A great change was to come over evangelical churches in the English-speaking world, largely as a result of the influence of Charles Finney. In 1824 he was ordained in the Presbyterian Church in New York State. He was a man of outstanding ability and very strong opinions who, if he had been willing to take more notice of some of the older and wiser ministers, could have been an outstanding asset to the church of God. We must, however, be careful before we blame Finney entirely. He was part of a movement which swept the north-east USA in the 1830s.

At first there was little indication of what was to come, other than Finney's use of what were called the 'new measures', e.g. the 'anxious seat',[6] and his criticisms of some of the older men who did not employ these new techniques. Like many others, Finney had been influenced by the 'spirit of the age'. New ideas were spreading into New England as a result of the Industrial Revolution and the French Revolution. It was very much 'out with the old and in with the new'. In a sense, those who were bringing in the new measures in the church were in line with this worldly spirit. During the course of the 1820s Finney developed a theology of revival as follows:

1. Revivals were not to be considered as sovereign acts of God: they could and should be promoted by men.
2. The doctrine of original sin, rendering man unable to receive the gospel, was emphatically denied.
3. Conversion was considered to be purely a question of the will, with which the Holy Spirit cooperates when a person decides for Christ. (One can see where much of the terminology of modern evangelism originated.)

4. Since conversion is not a result of a sovereign act of God in the new birth, all possible human means should be used to obtain it. Finney would press his congregation for decisions and ask them to stand up or come forward. Any preacher who did not press for immediate visible decisions was showing that he had no concern for the souls of his congregation.

Those in the churches who were not actively promoting revivals by the above means Finney considered to be delinquent and were severely censured. This censorious attitude was an evidence of Finney's pride. He had fallen into the 'snare of the devil' (1 Timothy 3:6–8, AV).

What were the results of Finney's teaching and methods? At first they seemed to produce results, but in the longer term they had the effect of quenching the Spirit, and the revivals which had formerly been so prevalent now began to die out. Initially, many of the older church leaders regarded the controversy as being just a question of one tradition against another. Partly because there was nothing much of Finney's in print at that time, they were unaware that Finney and his associates had embraced a new theology (really an old heresy). By the time they became aware of what had really taken place, the damage was done and in one sense it was too late.

'At the heart of the matter lay a different doctrine of conversion.'[7]

Many evangelicals believe that Finney was the architect of the Second Great Awakening in nineteenth-century America. However, when examined carefully, the facts seem to indicate otherwise. In the first place, Finney was only eight years old when the Second Great Awakening began in 1800. Like many others, he was used by God in the revivals of the 1820s and 1830s; but the revivals had been a feature of American church life for decades before Finney began to preach. He is also remarkably frank in his *Letters on Revival*, published in 1845. As Iain Murray says:

Chapter 18

Finney urged the need for caution against fanaticism, against using premature pressure for response, against fault-finding with churches and ministers: 'impulses' were not to be confused with the leading of the Spirit, and a greater teaching content was needed in preaching. By 'means and measures' it was possible to promote 'a certain kind of excitement' which is called 'a powerful revival of religion, but certainly not a revival of pure religion'. There are 'spurious revivals' in which 'many supposed converts are numbered, when in reality there is not a genuine convert among them'.

But the publication which has been widely read is not Finney's *Letters*, but his *Memoirs*, which give us a completely different picture. The frank admissions of the letters are wholly absent, and the world has been left with the false impression that Finney had introduced revival into church life, which had been previously characterized by formal evangelism-quenching Calvinism.

Revivalism in Britain

In the 1840s, partly due to literature and partly through visitors from America, revivalism seems to have spread to many parts of England and to a lesser extent to Wales and Scotland. After the initial enthusiasm, many became uneasy about endorsing the revivalist methods. Although initially welcoming revivalism, in 1843 the Congregational leader John Angell James referred to it as 'seductive and mischievous'.[8] The Wesleyan Methodists, concerned about the influence of the American Methodist revivalist James Caughey, requested in 1846 that he be recalled from Britain. In 1862, the Primitive Methodist John Simpson, comparing the 1859 Awakening with Revivalism wrote: '[The 1859 Awakening] seems to have come upon churches unawares, … it was not "got up", no revival-mongers were employed.'[9]

The 1857–58 revival

Although the earlier nineteenth-century awakenings in North America are not well known, the 1857/8 awakening which began in New York has

Revivals and revivalism

been more widely publicized. It began when Jeremiah Lanphier started special prayer meetings in Fulton Street, New York. This awakening was, however, not without its pedigree.

First of all, Lanphier had been a member of 19th Street Presbyterian Church and had sat under the ministry of James Alexander, the eldest son of Princeton Seminary's first professor. Alexander had lived through the 'new measures' controversy and was not in favour of Finney-style revivalism, but had experienced 'old-style' revivals during the 1820s and 1830s. Lanphier's prayer meetings were very much following the 'Concert of Prayer' approach. A second important factor at that time was a monetary collapse in October 1857 in New York, where some had lost millions at a stroke. There had also, according to Alexander, been a heightening of spiritual awareness in the months preceding the beginning of the Fulton Street prayer meetings.

The effects of those special prayer meetings were far-reaching. At first they were held weekly, but within a few weeks numbers had grown so much that Lanphier changed them to daily, and many others were held in other parts of New York. These prayer meetings were so numerous that the striking of the clock for twelve noon became known as the 'hour of prayer'. Alexander, who returned from a recuperation break in Europe in the spring of 1858, came back to be confronted by this remarkable movement of the Spirit of God. Several features of this revival are worth noting:

- Virtually all denominations were involved.
- At the peak of the revival, some prayer meetings were attended by thousands.
- Complete outsiders began to be converted during the prayer meetings.
- The prayer meetings had a marked absence of any 'excesses' or irreverence.
- Ministers began to be inundated by those seeking spiritual help.
- Sales of serious Christian books rocketed—the publisher of Spurgeon's sermons sold one hundred thousand.

Chapter 18

The awakening comes to Britain

Even before news of the New York Awakening had hit the shores of Britain, in the autumn of 1857 four young men began to meet for prayer in the old schoolhouse near Kells in County Antrim, Northern Ireland. During 1858, conversions began to be reported in the parish of Connor, and by the end of the year they were occurring every week. Connor churches soon became crowded to overflowing and crowds would on occasion listen to gospel preaching outside in the pouring rain. The powerful convicting work of the Holy Spirit would at times disrupt business. Groups of mill-workers sometimes came under conviction of sin and left their machines to pray. In Coleraine, the local paper delayed publication for a day because the compositors (type-setters) were seeking God in prayer.

About the same time and quite independently, Wales was also affected. Humphrey Jones, a Methodist minister, on returning from New York in 1858 brought news of the revival there. Jones and his friend David Morgan from the Calvinistic Methodist Church began to preach with great effect and the churches were quickened. Through the revival an estimated one hundred thousand people were converted to Christ.

In 1860 the revival crossed the channel from Antrim to the Ayrshire coast in Scotland and soon spread eastwards. Scotland was a land prepared. In 1839 there had been powerful revivals in Kilsyth and Dundee under the ministry of William Chalmers Burns. The Bonar brothers, Andrew and Horatius, had witnessed those awakenings and had maintained a prayerful and expectant spirit during the intervening years. Many preachers were used in Scotland during the revival, one of the most notable being Brownlow North. Nearly all of Scotland felt the impact of this work of God.

In England the revival proceeded in much the same way as it had done elsewhere, with united prayer meetings and powerful preaching. C. H. Spurgeon, the well-known Baptist minister in London commented in 1860: 'The times of refreshing from the presence of the Lord have at

Revivals and revivalism

last dawned upon our land. Everywhere there are signs of aroused activity and increased earnestness. A spirit of prayer is visiting our churches.'[10]

Although counting converts can be notoriously unreliable, reasonable estimates are that over the whole of the UK, by 1864 around one million[11] had been brought into the kingdom of Christ. Even parts of Southern Ireland were affected by the revival, including Dublin, Cork, and Kerry, where it was known as 'The Kerry Revival' because of the unusual blessing experienced there.

NOTES

1. Iain Murray, *Revival and Revivalism* (Edinburgh: Banner of Truth Trust, 1994), p. 51.
2. Evangelicalism in North America from 1750-1859 is a section of church history about which the Christian church has been largely ignorant, mainly due to a lack of published material. Iain Murray's book *Revival and Revivalism* goes a long way to correcting this deficit.
3. Murray, *Revival*, p. 125.
4. Murray, *Revival*, p. 127.
5. Habakkuk 2:14.
6. The 'anxious seat' was a place at the front of a church where, in response to the preaching, those seeking salvation were urged to come to publicly show their intention.
7. Murray, *Revival*, p. 244.
8. Murray, *Revival*, p. 393.
9. John Simpson, *Modern Revivals: Their Features and Incidents* (London: Richard Davies, 1862), pp. 10–14.
10. C. H. Spurgeon, *New Park Street Pulpit, 1860* (London: Alabaster and Passmore, 1861), preface.
11. The total population was around 20 million.

To the ends of the earth

When William Carey and his colleagues established the Christian mission at Serampore in India, they showed that the evangelization of the 'heathen' was possible, though often beset with difficulties and heartaches. The church as a whole was beginning to awaken to the 'Great Commission' (Matt. 28:18–20).

Although many of the Protestant nations of Europe joined in the task, the churches in the English-speaking world took the lead. There were several reasons for this. Firstly, God in his providence had included Britain in the sixteenth-century Reformation. Secondly, he had also lavished his grace on Britain and America by sending them wave after wave of spiritual awakenings in the seventeenth, eighteenth and nineteenth centuries. One direct result of these revivals in England and America was the increase in the number of candidates offering themselves to work as missionaries abroad. Thirdly, following the Napoleonic wars, Britain had become the number one maritime nation and was expanding her empire. This meant that Britain really did 'rule the waves'[1] and British missionaries could travel abroad with comparative ease to relocate around the empire.

Recent advances in the design of sailing ships to include improved steering, sails and underwater protection of hulls had also helped

A tea clipper

128 A Beginner's Guide to Church History

sea travel. Scientific instruments such as the compass and sextant were now available as essential tools for safer navigation. In the early nineteenth century, travel by ship around the world, although still not without its hazards, was becoming much more accessible. In 1869 the Suez Canal was opened, which significantly shortened journey times to India and the Far East. The tea clippers, too, plying between Britain and India or China, could achieve top speeds of around 17 knots (19.6 mph) and adjusted their routes to make good use of the trade winds.

Scottish missionaries

The Scottish churches were relatively late to take up the challenge of foreign missions. When they did engage with the task, they were to become among the leaders in European and American missionary work in India, sub-Saharan Africa, the West Indies, China and the New Hebrides. One of the best-known Scottish missionaries was the explorer David Livingstone, who opened up the interior of Africa. The lesser-known William Chalmers Burns was the first missionary to China from the Presbyterian Church in Scotland. He originally intended to travel to China in 1839, but was delayed by a revival in Kilsyth which began in the church where he was preaching. His twenty years in China (1847–68) were foundational to future work there.

Single women also played their part, one notable Scot being Mary Slessor in Calabar, West Africa. She soon began to adapt to the new environment: learning the Efik language, adopting a much more practical short hairstyle, and abandoning aspects of ladies' Victorian dress which were impractical for active work in a hot climate. As soon as she was able to, Mary began to teach the children and work in the dispensary. Many missionaries ate food which had been transported from Britain at considerable expense, but Mary opted for a more inexpensive local diet. This enabled her to save from her 'allowance' so as to support her mother and two sisters back in Dundee.

Chapter 19

Hazards and setbacks

In other cases mission work experienced great setbacks. One tragic example is that of the two missionaries John Williams and James Harris in the New Hebrides in the South Pacific. Williams and his wife and another missionary couple, commissioned by the London Missionary Society, had originally set sail for the New Hebrides in 1817. They had been well received on many of the Polynesian islands, and had established churches and translated the Bible into the Raratongan language. Sadly, in November 1839, when visiting the island of Erromango for the first time, John Williams and James Harris were clubbed to death and eaten by the locals: an abrupt and brutal end to the lives of two very productive Christian missionaries. Many of the inhabitants of other islands were grief-stricken when they heard the news. There is, however, a rather wonderful sequel to this story. In the 170 years since the murder of Williams and Harris, a thriving church has been established on Erromango; so much so that in 2009, relatives of those first cannibals invited all known relatives of John Williams from around the world to come to a special celebration including the renaming of the bay as 'Williams Bay'. A remarkable triumph for the Christian gospel!

Hudson Taylor and inland China

Perhaps the most well-known example of gospel advance in the nineteenth century is connected with James Hudson Taylor and the China Inland Mission. Born in Barnsley in 1832 into a godly Methodist home, Hudson Taylor expressed a desire even as a young child to be a missionary to China. The outworking of this desire has had repercussions well beyond his or anyone else's wildest dreams. Historian Ruth Tucker summarizes the theme of his life: 'No other missionary in the nineteen centuries since the Apostle Paul ... has carried out a more systematized plan of evangelizing a broad geographical area than Hudson Taylor.'[2]

But there was not a smooth transition between his childhood aspirations and adult life. During his teens he turned away from his earlier childhood faith, but was then converted at the age of nineteen through reading an evangelistic tract. It was not long after this that he embarked on training for missionary work abroad, including studies in medicine, and offered himself to the Chinese Evangelization Society (CES). Some two years later, in September 1853, a small three-masted clipper, the *Dumfries*, slipped quietly out of Liverpool harbour with the twenty-one-year-old Hudson Taylor aboard. His mother's last view of him was as a tiny figure, standing on the ship's cross-trees, waving his hat as the ship disappeared from view. At that time, China was just coming into the Christian West's consciousness; only a few dozen missionaries were stationed there.

Five months after leaving Liverpool, Hudson Taylor's ship arrived in Shanghai to be greeted by a civil war. This made life very difficult for missionaries. In addition, the CES had not sent any money to Hudson, so he had to eke out his own meagre resources and rely on the help of other Europeans. Despite these difficulties, within months of arriving, with the native language still a challenge, Hudson and another missionary set off inland, sailing up the Huangpu River and distributing Chinese Bibles and tracts. Hudson soon began to realize that European attire was a distinct disadvantage—the missionaries stood out like sore thumbs. The problem was that many veteran missionaries wore European dress and disapproved of dressing like the locals.

In late 1855, Hudson Taylor met William Burns, who had been in China for eight years. The two men worked together for some time and each

Chapter 19

benefited from the other. Burns passed on the good advice that, when starting work in a new town, it was best to visit the back streets and tea rooms rather than the town centre or the market place. For his part, when Hudson decided to adopt Chinese dress, Burns followed suit. Hudson was also impressed with the godliness of his companion, particularly his prayer life. Circumstances were such that after around a year together they parted company.

By 1857, the CES had been so unreliable in supporting Hudson Taylor that he decided to resign from the mission and work as an independent missionary. He had up until then been able to provide some income for himself by working as a doctor and had also received support from a wealthy friend in England. He then joined another doctor and moved to Ningbo to set up a hospital there. At Ningbo he met and in 1858 married Maria Dyer, daughter of deceased missionaries. By 1860, mainly due to overwork, Hudson Taylor's health began to deteriorate. The following year he became seriously ill (probably with hepatitis) and was forced to return to England to recover. His wife Maria and their daughter Gracie came with him.

While in England he was able to re-evaluate the situation in China with a view to expanding the work inland. First of all he completed his medical studies and qualified in July 1862. He also worked on the translation of the New Testament into Chinese, using a Romanized alphabet.[3] This would be particularly useful to missionaries, who learned to speak the language but struggled to master the thousands of Chinese characters. Hudson was becoming more well known in Britain and was asked to speak at an increasing number of meetings around the country. By mid 1865 he had come to the conviction that the way forward for the evangelization of inland China was to form a new interdenominational mission, the China Inland Mission (CIM), devoted to that task. In June of that year the first CIM bank account was opened. Just one year later, on 26 May 1866, the first group of seventeen CIM missionaries set sail for China on the *Lammermuir*. In addition there were now four Taylor children, making

To the ends of the earth

a total of twenty-one in their party. After four months, having survived two violent typhoons in the South China Sea, they docked at Shanghai.

Between the first arrival of CIM missionaries in China and Hudson Taylor's death in 1905, he spent most of his time in China, but also travelled back to Europe and America to resolve problems and further expand the work. During his lifetime alone, the CIM was responsible for sending nearly nine hundred missionaries to China and establishing mission centres in all eighteen provinces. These numbers of recruits could never have been realized apart from the revivals in Britain and America in 1857–60. Primarily because of the CIM's opposition to the opium trade, Hudson Taylor has been regarded as one of the most significant Europeans to visit China in the nineteenth century. He was able to preach in several Chinese languages, including Mandarin, Chaozhou, and the Wu dialects of Shanghai and Ningbo. The last of these he knew well enough to help prepare a colloquial edition of the New Testament.

The missionaries covered in this chapter are but a few of a great army of gospel workers. As well as a host of the less well-known overseas workers, other more famous names include Henry Martyn, who brought the gospel to much of the Middle East, Adoniram and Ann Judson of Burma, and James Fraser, who went to the Lisu tribes between Burma and China. But perhaps the most remarkable of all missionary endeavours was the establishing of the Church in Korea, which is the subject of our next chapter.

NOTES

1 In 1810 Britain had close to 1000 ships flying the Royal Navy's White Ensign flag.
2 Ruth Tucker, *From Jerusalem to Irian Jaya: A Biographical History of Christian Missions* (Grand Rapids: Zondervan, 1983), p. 73.
3 This version of Chinese is sometimes referred to as Pinyin.

Born in adversity

In 1866, the year that the first CIM missionaries set sail for China, the Welshman Robert Thomas sailed on the American ship *General Sherman* from China to Korea. The main purpose of the ship's visit was to initiate trade links with the Koreans, but Robert Thomas' aim was, if possible, to begin gospel work there. It had become known that many Koreans were literate and could read Chinese characters, so Thomas was armed with Chinese Bibles and tracts.

The ship crossed the Yellow Sea from China and steamed the sixty-eight miles up the Taedong river to the walled city of Pyongyang (now the capital of North Korea). At that time, some ocean-going vessels could only reach that far upriver on the twice-monthly 'spring' high tide.[1] The captain and crew were unaware of this fact, which was to have a disastrous effect on their mission. While the American and European members of the 'trade mission' went ashore to make contact with the authorities, some members of the Chinese/Malay crew kidnapped several Koreans. This provoked a fight between those on the ship and some of the Koreans on the shore, who were armed with flintlock rifles. Because the ship had heavier weapons, this exchange of fire resulted in casualties ashore. With the situation becoming increasingly dangerous, the captain decided to withdraw downstream, but the ship ran aground in shallow water. The Koreans then loaded several small boats with tinder-dry brushwood, linked them together and set fire to the brush. They then manoeuvred this chain of fire ships so that they drifted towards the stranded *General Sherman*, setting it on fire so that it had to be abandoned. As the visitors attempted to wade ashore they were attacked and killed by the hostile locals. Thomas was no exception, apart from the fact that while he was being attacked he offered no resistance but handed out his armful of Bibles and tracts. Much of this literature

Born in adversity

was confiscated by the authorities, but some was concealed and read later. Some twenty-seven years later, one of the first converts revealed that his father had kept and read one of Thomas' Bibles.

First Korean Christians

It was not until 1893 that the first churches were founded in Pyongyang. American Methodists and Presbyterians began work there at the same time. Those Bibles given out earlier by Robert Thomas were now beginning to bear fruit. Small churches were soon established, but no sooner had they sprung up than the city became the centre of a conflict between Chinese and Japanese armies. (Korea's history in modern times has been punctuated by wars between foreign armies conducted on Korean soil.) The missionaries were withdrawn for their own safety and the Christian believers retreated into the hills. When the fighting ceased, both Korean believers and missionaries returned. The Koreans brought news of small churches being formed where they had been scattered during the fighting. A 'Macedonian call'[2] for reinforcements went back to the USA, and other workers soon came to help. The early twentieth century proved to be a rich harvest time for the growing Korean churches. In addition, in 1907 an in-depth revival took place in these young churches and there were great increases in the numbers of believers. One of the outstanding features of this revival was the spontaneous public confession of sins by many in the churches. Some of the missionaries were wary of this development but had to recognize that these effects were not man-made, but evidence of a deep work of conviction by the Holy Spirit which was preparing the church for the severe persecutions to come.

Immediately following the revival in 1907 there was another war on the Korean peninsula, this time between Russia and Japan. As the lesser of two evils, the Koreans were happy for Japanese forces to advance northwards to drive the Russians out of their country. At the cessation of hostilities there was a desire for independence, as Bruce Hunt writes:

Chapter 20

The country wanted a leader and the Christian Church was the strongest, most influential single organization in Korea. Had she departed even a little from the strict principle of non-interference in politics, thousands would have welcomed her leadership ...We might have again witnessed the 'cross of Constantine' leading a great army. I believe that Korea, like the Roman Empire, would have adopted Christianity in a day, ... and we would have had another Roman Church.[3]

Persecution under Japanese rule

The desire for independence was unrealized, and the Japanese remained in occupation. This was to lead to persecution of the church. One of the most serious causes of this persecution was the introduction by the Japanese in the 1930s of mandatory homage to ancestors at Shinto shrines. This requirement is reminiscent of 'emperor worship' in the early church. Some in the churches rationalized this activity as merely a 'patriotic' formality, but many Christians refused to comply and were penalized by imprisonment and torture. The Japanese did not execute people for refusing to submit to shrine worship: they just imprisoned them and many died as a result of their incarceration. As Bruce Hunt says, 'death came as a result of torture, malnutrition, exposure, disease and illness in prison, not execution'.[4]

'No-one ... knows, or will ever know, the number and names of all those who died as a result of their testimony against shrine worship.'[5]

The Japanese remained in control of the country until they were defeated by the Americans at the end of the Second World War. Unfortunately, during the final phase of the war, Chinese Communist troops took advantage of Japanese forces retreating, and moved in to occupy the north of the Korean peninsula. The Yalta Agreement at the end of the war in 1945 left the country divided between opposing regimes. After the

Born in adversity

war, in South Korea the Christian church grew to become, by 1999, the majority religion of that country. Although cults and extremists form part of that statistic, evangelicals were predominant among those professing to be Christian. In the early twenty-first century, Korean pastors coming to study in the UK would refer to large churches with as many as five pastors being commonplace. In recent times, South Korea has been the number one nation sending missionaries out to the rest of the world. When asked the secret of the Korean church's success, one such pastor replied that he considered one important factor to be the daily early-morning prayer meetings.

Since the Communist takeover, the church in North Korea has been relentlessly persecuted by the State and it is difficult to establish what is really happening to God's people there. Is the hour of their deliverance near at hand? The church in the 'free' world should be praying for this.

NOTES

1 'Spring' high tides are the high water level when the moon is full or new and exerts its maximum pull on the oceans. 'Neap' high tides are the much lower high water level at new moon.
2 See Acts 16:9.
3 Bruce Hunt, *The Korean Pentecost* (Edinburgh: Banner of Truth Trust, 1977, repr. 2015), pp. 73–74.
4 Hunt, *Korean Pentecost*, p. 157.
5 Hunt, *Korean Pentecost*, p. 113.

Testing times

While the missionary movement in other parts of the world was making great advances for the gospel, in late nineteenth-century Europe and America the church began to experience a concerted counter-attack, particularly on the truth of Scripture.

Although the Bible has never been without its critics, even from within the pale of the professing church,[1] an increasing number of them arose in Europe during the nineteenth century. This thinking had undoubtedly been influenced by the secular philosophy behind the French Revolution (1789). Three main areas came under attack: the historicity and morality of the Old Testament, the writings of the Apostle Paul, and the deity, miracles and bodily resurrection of Christ. Having been weakened by the Arminian theology[2] and decision-based evangelism introduced by Charles Finney, many churches were unprepared for what was to come. Like all errors and heresies, these so-called 'liberal' views of the Bible came in by degrees. But by the early decades of the twentieth century many of these 'critical' views of Scripture were being introduced into the denominational training colleges and university theological faculties. The result was that the gospel message was gradually being watered down and modified so that it ended up as 'another gospel' (Gal. 1:6–9).

Even some of those holding to a more robust Calvinism were severely tested. The American theologian Gresham Machen, during a time of study in Germany, found liberal views hard to resist, particularly with a teacher he felt exemplified Christian devotion. As Machen's biographer, Ned Stonehouse, writes: '[Professor] Hermann made Liberalism wonderfully attractive and heart-gripping. This he did not so much by the plausibility of intellectual argument as by the magnetic and overpowering force of his fervent religious spirit.'[3]

Thankfully Machen was able to recover from this temptation and his experiences are described by Terry A. Chrisope in his book, *Towards a Sure Faith*.[4] In 1929 Machen went on to be one of the founders of Westminster Theological Seminary, following the lapse of Princeton Theological Seminary into liberalism.

Charles Darwin's *Origin of Species*

Another area of attack upon the validity of the Bible emanated from Charles Darwin's *Origin of Species*, which was published in 1859. Many within the churches in the English-speaking world were completely unprepared for the challenge which came from this quarter. Some Bible scholars felt that they should somehow try to accommodate Darwin's 'millions of years' timescale with the very much shorter thousands of years required by a straightforward reading of the early chapters of the book of Genesis. But they were no match for their atheistic opponents. In the intervening 150 years, Darwinism and an evolutionary mind-set has increasingly dominated 'Western' thinking. Those who espouse the six-day special creation view of origins are likely to be despised and ridiculed, and even discriminated against in their field of scientific expertise.

Since the publication of Darwin's thesis, however, several scientific developments have arisen which seriously challenge his theory. In his speculations of how different species were related to each other, Darwin did not have access to more recent work in the field of genetics which points to a completely different model. He was also working with very limited data, being only aware of 15% of the species which have now been discovered.[5] Several organizations have been recently set up to study, evaluate and, where appropriate, refute evolutionary ideas. Creationists have rightly exposed the fact that 'evolution' is a philosophical view of origins, not a science.

Chapter 21

Orthodox protests

At the time, there were voices raised against these trends. C. H. Spurgeon, the Baptist pastor of the Metropolitan Tabernacle in London, warned against embracing the new Bible-denigrating views. In the *Sword and Trowel* (April 1887), Spurgeon wrote: 'We are glad that the article upon "The Down Grade" has excited notice ... Our warfare is with men who are giving up the atoning sacrifice, denying the inspiration of Holy Scripture, and casting slurs upon justification by faith.' Controversy

Charles Haddon Spurgeon

developed, and Spurgeon became the focal point of criticism. The Baptist Union, which was bitterly divided over the question, ultimately voted to censure him. One of the jibes which 'liberals' would hurl at preachers who spoke of the blood of Christ was that they were preaching a 'butcher-shop religion'.

In the Church of England, J. C. Ryle maintained an orthodox evangelical stance, despite the defections from that position among his contemporaries. Ryle, in his writings, makes it quite clear where he stands: 'The sceptical writers against Moses and the Pentateuch have greatly erred. Let us stand fast and not doubt that every word in the Old Testament, as well as the New, was given by inspiration of God.'[6]

John Charles Ryle

But with so many adopting the new unbiblical doctrines, the future of the true church of God looked bleak in both Europe and America.

The Brethren movement

There were, however, some sections of the church which were not contaminated by the 'liberal' heresy. One of the largest of these was the Brethren. This was a movement which began in the 1820s, largely from within the Church of England. In essence, the Brethren were attempting to address the age-old problem of the incomplete reformation of the Church of England. As if in anticipation of the departure from Scripture which was soon to become widespread, the Brethren were characterized by a back-to-the-Bible mentality, and consequently the 'liberal theology' revolution left them virtually untouched. Although Brethrenism was never uniform, the following are some of the main features of the movement:

- A firm commitment to Scripture as the church's sole authority.
- A personal experience of conversion essential to being a true Christian.
- A rejection of all forms of clericalism: each 'assembly'[7] was independently governed by a plurality of elders.
- Those with teaching and preaching gifts were encouraged to use them, but there were no salaried pastors.
- Only believers' baptism was practised.
- Practical godliness in the home was considered to be important—children and servants were included in daily family worship.
- Evangelism and overseas missionary work had a high priority.
- The principle of separation from the world and all deviant expressions of Christianity was expected, although this often varied between different groups and families.
- Acceptance of a pre-millennial[8] view of biblical prophecy. (Had they known the source of this view, many might have been less enthusiastic in embracing it.)[9]

Chapter 21

Theologically, the Brethren accepted Protestant orthodoxy, but most held the Arminian views of the Wesleyan Methodists.

Outstanding men in the Brethren movement included the philanthropist George Müller and the missionary to China, Hudson Taylor.

Strict Baptists

Another group that refused to 'move with the times' was the Strict and Particular Baptists. These believers have often been misunderstood and misrepresented because of their Calvinistic beliefs and practice of restricted communion (baptized believers only). Yet in the late nineteenth century when the majority in other sections of Protestantism were departing from the faith, they held the line. At that time many new Strict Baptist churches were also being planted all over England.

William Carey, the recognized 'father' of the modern missionary movement, had been sent to India by the Particular Baptists of Northamptonshire (see chapter 17). Partly because Carey's work in Serampore eventually merged with the General Baptists, the Strict Baptist Mission was founded in India in 1861, supported by the growing number of Strict Baptist churches in England.[10]

When evangelical recovery came in the mid-twentieth century, pastors and members from the Strict Baptist Churches played an important role in expanding and deepening the work of God in Britain.

***

As is always the case, in times of spiritual decline God is also at work. With many in the churches of Europe and America succumbing to the liberal heresy, the Lord was building his church in the Far East (e.g. Korea and China: see chapters 19 and 20). But there was also to be another positive development in the UK.

Testing times

The Welsh Revival 1904–5

The roots of this awakening go back into the 1890s. Firstly, two pastors from Newquay and Aberaeron in West Wales, Joseph Jenkins and his nephew John Thickens, met regularly for prayer for personal and national revival. Secondly, two evangelistic agencies, the Salvation Army (founded in 1870) and the Forward Movement of the Calvinistic Methodists, were active in evangelism and church planting. Thirdly, the Keswick Movement, though not without its errors,[11] emphasized the need for believers to know a greater measure of the Holy Spirit in their personal experience. As early as 1900, initial stirrings occurred in Trinity Calvinistic Methodist Church in Tonypandy, with six hundred being converted by late 1904. Other places similarly affected were Barmouth (1902), Anglesey and Towyn.

The revival gathered momentum in 1904, mainly in connection with several young peoples' conferences. It was in September, during the early-morning prayer time at one of these conferences at Blaenanerch, that Evan Roberts prayed for the Holy Spirit to 'bend' him. It was a defining moment for him personally, and for the revival. Roberts returned to his home town of Loughor, where his family were wonderfully awakened. From this time, Roberts assumed unofficial leadership of the revival. He made several tours of Wales with a small choir of young women. Prayer, singing and testimonies dominated the meetings. There was very little preaching. Revival usually broke out where he went, but it was not restricted to places he visited, and had begun to occur in parts of Wales even before he was 'awakened'.

The 1904 Revival was a mixed affair, as most revivals are, but it included a genuine work of God which had lasting effects. Many notorious drunkards and criminals were changed and some became gospel preachers. Miners in Glamorgan held prayer meetings underground, and their pit ponies had to be 're-educated' to respond to their cleaned-up language!

The Welsh Revival had a surprising international effect. Welsh communities and missionaries around the world were affected, notably

A Beginner's Guide to Church History **143**

Chapter 21

in north-east India, Madagascar and Patagonia. Many European countries were also influenced, including parts of France, Germany, Belgium, Norway, Sweden and the Balkans. They experienced spiritual blessing on hearing of events in Wales. Parts of Africa were also affected, particularly in the south.

NOTES

1 Marcion (second century) cut out 'unwanted' passages from the Old Testament.

2 '…anti-Calvinism … had emasculated the churches'. John McDonald, *Grace to the Nations* (Abingdon: Grace Baptist Mission, 2011), p. 8.

3 N. B. Stonehouse, *J. Gresham Machen: a biographical memoir* (Edinburgh: Banner of Truth Trust, 1987), p. 105.

4 Terry A. Chrisope, *Towards a Sure Faith* (Fearn: Christian Focus Publications, 2000).

5 Nathaniel Jeanson, *Replacing Darwin: the new origin of species* (Green Forest, AR: Master Books, 2018).

6 J. C. Ryle, *Expository Thoughts on John* (many editions available), commenting on John 5:45–47.

7 Until the late twentieth century, the Brethren religiously avoided the use of the word 'church'; they referred to their local group as an 'assembly'.

8 Premillennialism teaches that Christ's second coming will precede a literal 1000-year reign on earth, which will be followed by a brief falling away and the final judgement.

9 The modern premillennial interpretation of prophecy almost certainly originated at the Counter-Reformation from a Spanish Jesuit called Ribera. For a fuller discussion of this issue see the author's *History Revealed in Advance* (2017), chapter 6. (ISBN 978-0-244-30862-9.)

10 John MacDonald, *Grace to the Nations* (Abingdon: Grace Baptist Mission, 2011), p. 11.

11 The late-nineteenth-century Keswick Movement can be viewed as a reaction to the weak view of conversion which had come into the churches from Finney's teachings (see chapter 18). Keswick teaching urged such 'carnal' Christians to seek an experience of full surrender leading to higher or deeper spiritual life.

Redefining the boundaries

In the early years of the twentieth century, there was a mood of optimism in the West. During the preceding one hundred years there had been great strides of progress in many areas. Sanitation had been improved, and with it general health. Advances in medicine meant that patients could have surgery under anaesthetic. Advances in the field of electrical science meant that electricity was available in many homes and was being introduced to power the trams. Gas was also widely used for lighting and heating. The steam engine had powered expanding railway networks. In the 1890s, the internal combustion engine had been developed, and motor vehicles were appearing on the roads. Postal services were available to all, and same-day deliveries were available from London to other major cities in the UK. In Britain, the Education Act of 1870 made education both compulsory and free. Despite many ongoing social, political and health issues, life for the majority was becoming more comfortable and prosperous.

Within the orbit of the mainstream Protestant churches there was also an optimistic spirit, and with good reason. The gospel advance around the world during the nineteenth century had been nothing short of phenomenal. In many countries this was continuing and new people groups were being reached. But many within the major Protestant denominations seemed unaware of the doctrinal declension which had been creeping into the churches as more and more leaders embraced the new doctrines of liberal theology. Others regarded this shifting theological climate as progress away from the divisive dogmas of earlier generations.

The 1910 Edinburgh Missionary Conference

The idea of holding a missionary conference to improve cooperation between those from different denominations involved in missionary work

Chapter 22

was something that William Carey would have approved of. One hundred years after Carey, the concept of those from different missions meeting to confer seemed even more appealing. But with so many changes having taken place within the Protestant churches, the 1910 Edinburgh Conference was completely different from anything Carey could have envisaged.

Invitation to participate in the conference seems to have been on the following rather arbitrary basis:

1. No distinctive doctrinal standards were required for attendance. On the other hand, no Roman Catholic or Eastern Orthodox delegates were invited.
2. A delegation from the 'High Church' party of the Church of England was present. Bishop Ryle, who died in 1901, would have opposed this. In his day he had spoken out strongly against the High Church 'Tractarian Movement'.[1]
3. Because missions were invited to send delegates on the basis of their minimum annual spending, this automatically excluded several small evangelical missions working in South America.[2]

In Carey's time, the Protestant missions still held to seventeenth-century confessional standards: the Westminster Confession, the Savoy Declaration and the 1689 Baptist Confession. Edinburgh shows how much the major denominational missions had departed from their evangelical roots. Partly because of its inclusivism, the Edinburgh Conference has been considered by many to be the forerunner of the World Council of Churches, established some three decades later in 1948.

The optimism of the early twentieth century in both church and state was rudely shattered by the First World War, the most extensive conflict which the world had ever seen. It was modern warfare with a vengeance, using tanks, machine guns, aircraft and bombs. The effect on the Protestant churches was devastating. After the war, many 'lost their faith' because it had no sure biblical foundation, and church attendances plummeted. Although few were aware of it, the severe testing of the conflict had served to expose the shallowness of many whose 'faith' was the product of the defective ideas of theological liberalism.

Martyn Lloyd-Jones

But as in all previous dark eras of the church's history, God had not forgotten his people. Soon after war was declared, a young Welsh lad, Martyn Lloyd-Jones, then in his early teens, was helping his father with a milk delivery business in Westminster in his spare time. By the autumn of 1916, he had been accepted as a medical student at St Bartholomew's Hospital in the city of London. He was an outstanding student and after passing his medical exams he began to work with Sir Thomas Horder, one of Britain's leading physicians.

Although as yet unconverted, Lloyd-Jones was typical of many churchgoers of his generation who thought that they were Christians. Lloyd-Jones himself later reflected on the kind of preaching which had helped to produce this mind-set: 'The preaching we had was always based on the assumption that we [churchgoers] were all Christians. What I needed was preaching that would convict me of sin and make me see my need.'[3]

Several factors would bring about a change. Firstly, several adverse 'providences' had made him feel that 'here have we no continuing city'.[4] He had escaped from a house fire at the age of ten, and his father had recently experienced bankruptcy, resulting in the family having to move into temporary accommodation several times. Secondly, visiting Dr Horder's wealthy patients made him realize that man's physical maladies were often related to the deeper spiritual malady—sin. Thirdly, he was given a booklet on the life of the eighteenth-century evangelical preacher Howell Harris. All three factors conspired together so that by 1925 Lloyd-Jones was brought to see that 'my trouble was not only that I did things that were wrong, but that I, myself, was wrong at the very centre of my being'.[5]

Chapter 22

His conversion resulted in him discovering within himself a desire to serve God as a preacher, a healer of men's souls rather than their bodies. Consequently, one weekend at the end of November 1926 saw Lloyd-Jones on the train from London to Port Talbot in South Wales. He had been invited to preach at the Bethlehem Forward Movement Church in the Sandfields district of the town. Though by then he had probably only preached around a dozen times, the congregation welcomed him with open arms and, as a result of that one visit, called him to be their pastor. Martyn and his fiancée, Bethan, were married early in the new year (1927) and after a brief honeymoon in Torquay moved into the manse in Sandfields. It was recognized to be a difficult place for gospel work, yet despite a continued haemorrhaging in church attendance nationwide, congregations began to grow under the young Lloyd-Jones' ministry. After a few years there was a steady stream of converts. By the end of 1930, membership of the church had more than doubled, with forty-four being baptized on a single occasion in November that year. This rising tide of spiritual blessing reached its peak in 1931, and was considered, by those who could remember, to be as much a revival as events in 1904/5. Among the converts that year were notorious local people whose changed lives were evident for all to see.[6]

As well as the work in Sandfields, Lloyd-Jones soon received invitations to preach all over Wales, mainly during weekdays, plus making two preaching visits to North America. After a few years, he also found that his medical ability became in demand, and he gave

D. Martyn Lloyd-Jones

advice free of charge. This increased workload eventually began to tell on 'the Doctor', and he came to the conclusion that he could not continue without it causing a breakdown. 'His present heavy duties had become a physical burden to him and he did not see how he could fulfil his ministry satisfactorily if he continued.'[7]

The invitation to take up a pastorate in London seemed a solution to the problem, and eventually in May 1938 he was asked by Dr Campbell-Morgan to come to Westminster Chapel as his assistant. A year later, he accepted the call to be associate pastor during Campbell-Morgan's closing years of ministry at Westminster.

Evangelism in Eastern Europe

James Alexander Stewart was born in Glasgow in 1910. He began public preaching at the age of 14, and worked for the Open-Air Mission as an evangelist along the border between England and Scotland until 1933. In 1934 he began to work as an independent evangelist on the continent of Europe, starting in Latvia, where he was associated with Pastor William Fetler.[8] In 1935 Stewart extended his mission work to Poland and Estonia, and then to Czechoslovakia in 1936. While working in Czechoslovakia during 1937–38, he occasionally made missionary trips to Hungary. In 1938, on one of his visits into Hungary, he met and married Ruth Mahan, a Southern Baptist missionary, who from that time on became his faithful companion and colleague in his evangelistic efforts. He was well received by evangelical churches in Eastern Europe and significant numbers were converted under his ministry. Even in the late twentieth century, some believers from Eastern Europe could remember Stewart's contribution to the growth of the churches there in the 1930s. This influx of converts just before the Second World War meant that the churches were strengthened to withstand the persecution which arose when those countries came under Communist rule at the end of the war.

Chapter 22

NOTES

1 The nineteenth-century Tractarian Movement was from within the Church of England, aiming to introduce Roman Catholic practices and rituals into the Church's liturgy. Several of the early Tractarian leaders eventually joined the Church of Rome

2 A number of leading evangelicals connected with these South American evangelical missions were disturbed by their exclusion from the conference. In response, in 1911 the Evangelical Union of South America (EUSA) was formed.

3 Iain H Murray, *D. Martyn Lloyd-Jones: the First Forty Years* (Edinburgh: Banner of Truth Trust, 1982), p. 58.

4 Hebrews 13:14, AV.

5 Murray, *First Forty Years*, p. 64.

6 Bethan Lloyd-Jones, *Memories of Sandfields* (Edinburgh: Banner of Truth Trust, 2008).

7 Murray, *First Forty Years*, pp. 334–335.

8 William Fetler was a Latvian Baptist pastor, who had trained at Spurgeon's College and had also had connections with Evan Roberts shortly after the Welsh Revival of 1904. He had carried out effective evangelistic missions in Eastern Europe, particularly among Russian POWs during the First World War.

Evangelical recovery

Just one week after 'Victory in Europe' on 8 May 1945, Dr Campbell-Morgan, the recently-retired minister of Westminster Chapel, passed into eternity. Two years earlier, Martyn Lloyd-Jones, who had been Campbell Morgan's associate for four years, was invited to take up the position as sole minister. At that time, friends and church leaders in Wales tried to persuade Lloyd-Jones to return to the Principality, but after due consideration and much heart-searching, he decided to remain at Westminster Chapel. Neither he nor anyone else could have envisaged the great benefit to the cause of Christ to which this decision would lead.

Lloyd-Jones the preacher

In the immediate post-war years, the main task for Lloyd-Jones at Westminster Chapel was to 'rebuild' the congregation. The end of the war meant that some members moved away out of London. Many of the more elderly who remained would still have preferred the preaching style and content of the late Campbell Morgan to that of Lloyd-Jones. The latter was decidedly Calvinistic and 'Puritan' in his approach to preaching, and there was more theology in his sermons than had been true of those of his predecessors. One of the newly-elected deacons described his preaching as, 'the Puritans in brand-new suits.' John Owen, Richard Baxter and Jonathan Edwards were some of his favourite sources, but he endeavoured to win over those in his congregation to whom Reformed theology sounded strange, if not alien. It was not long before his ministry began to bear fruit. In the end-of-year report for 1946, he was able to say, 'The steady increase in the size of the congregation, both morning and evening, has been noticeable ... above all else we rejoice in the fact that God has been pleased to bless the preaching of the word to the conversion of many souls.'[1]

Chapter 23

Conversions under Lloyd-Jones' ministry were entirely consistent with the fact that he saw himself primarily as an evangelist.[2] Numbers attending the services continued to increase steadily until by May 1948 the lower gallery at the chapel was reopened, initially for an evening service. By the mid-1950s, Sunday attendances rose to more than fifteen hundred. Lloyd-Jones made it known that if any wanted to, they could come to his vestry and speak personally with him after the evening service. Mr Micklewright, one of his deacons, described these enquirers as 'wounded birds'. Because consecutive expository preaching[3] was virtually unknown at that time, even in evangelical churches, Lloyd-Jones only introduced it gradually.

For the Friday evening meeting, in 1944 he began a discussion time. Many found these discussions helpful in steering them away from their previously-held errors, and into the truth. Attendance at these meetings was initially around seventy-five, but had risen to two hundred by late 1947. During the late 1940s, Lloyd-Jones replaced these discussions with a verse-by-verse Bible study series on the book of Romans. This series continued for nearly twenty years until serious illness intervened. By that time he had reached the first part of chapter 14. The whole of the Romans series (fourteen volumes) has been published in English. Many of Lloyd-Jones' sermons have been translated into other languages—French, Spanish, Portuguese, Romanian[4] and Chinese, to name but a few.

As well as his ministry at Westminster Chapel, Lloyd-Jones preached in other parts of the UK mid-week. He also preached in Wales, Europe, Canada, the USA and South Africa during his summer breaks.

Lloyd-Jones the 'encourager'

Many will associate Martyn Lloyd-Jones just with his ministry in London, but he also had a much wider sphere of influence, encouraging other individuals and groups to pursue their own particular ministries.

Evangelical recovery

ENCOURAGING STUDENTS

In the 1940s, Lloyd-Jones took an active interest in the work of the Inter Varsity Fellowship (IVF). He could wholeheartedly support this cause because of its solid stand for scripture and doctrine, which he had encouraged. For several years he chaired the committee for the International Fellowship of Evangelical Students (IFES), spoke at the IFES conference, and was involved with the Christian Medical Fellowship (CMF). Among other new ventures which Lloyd-Jones encouraged were the IVF-sponsored Summer Schools in Wales during the late 1940s. These eventually metamorphosed into the Evangelical Movement of Wales, with its conferences, youth camps and literature ministry. His influence on the student world is best described in Iain Murray's words:

'This first European Conference of the IFES [in 1948] gave an impulse to minds and hearts which was to bear fruit in churches and mission fields across the world. But ... no one yet imagined the extent to which the international influence of [Lloyd-Jones'] ministry would grow.'[5]

ENCOURAGING PASTORS

During the war years, a small group of evangelical ministers met quarterly in London at Westminster Chapel for mutual encouragement. Naturally they looked to Lloyd-Jones as their leader. The format of the meeting was generally reporting on their own situations followed by discussion of a chosen relevant issue. With the passage of time, this meeting, eventually called the Westminster Fellowship, grew to several hundred and included men from many denominations. Pastors found the fellowship to be invaluable, particularly as some felt increasingly isolated in mixed denominations.

Another important venture during the 1940s was the establishment in London of an evangelical college for ministerial training. When

Chapter 23

London Bible College was duly settled in its permanent home in 1946, Ernest Kevan, formerly a Strict Baptist pastor, was its first principal, at Lloyd-Jones' recommendation. As Iain Murray says, 'The college's close links with Westminster Chapel were to be a means of far-reaching influence.'[6]

A third agency which proved to be of help to many was the Puritan Conference. This two-day conference, held mid-week in December, arose out of a revived interest among Oxford graduates in the teaching of the seventeenth-century Puritans. The first conference was held in 1950 under the general title, 'The Distinctive Theological Contribution of the English Puritans.'[7] Around twenty attended that first conference, but interest soon grew until numbers would often be over two hundred. The conference still continues today, nearly seventy years later, under the revised name of the Westminster Conference.

Literary ventures

The Evangelical Library, first 'launched' in 1943, really began when its founder was converted in a Strict Baptist Chapel in Brighton in 1903. After his conversion, and encouraged by his pastor, J. K. Popham, Geoffrey Williams developed an interest in Reformed and Puritan books, many of which had been popular in earlier times but were now out of print. He not only read these largely-forgotten authors, but began collecting copies from second-hand bookshops. By the time he was introduced to Lloyd-Jones, just before the Second World War, Geoffrey Williams was operating a lending library of some twenty-five thousand books from his home in Surrey. As soon as he saw this unique collection of books, Lloyd-Jones felt that it should have a much wider access to the Christian world. In consequence, in 1943 the library was moved to Chiltern Street in Marylebone and opened there as the Evangelical Library. The library has continued over seventy-five years to provide a valuable resource for pastors, preachers and Christian writers.

Another literary venture which used the library's resources was the Banner of Truth Trust. The Trust came into being in 1957 when Iain Murray, then Lloyd-Jones' assistant at Westminster Chapel, was brought into contact with the successful businessman Jack Cullum.[8] The result was an ambitious publishing venture for 'the advancement of historic and Calvinistic Christianity'. The republication of long-forgotten Christian classics, eagerly snapped up by a hungry readership, gave rise to 'a whole school of literature to which a superficial evangelicalism had long been oblivious'.[9] To date, the Trust has published more than one thousand titles, and some have been translated into several languages.

NOTES

1. Iain H Murray, *D. Martyn Lloyd-Jones: the Fight of Faith* (Edinburgh: Banner of Truth Trust, 1990), p.166.
2. Letter to Peter Golding, *Congregational Concern Magazine*, Autumn 1999, p.5.
3. Consecutive expository preaching is the exposition of the whole of a portion of the Bible (one or more chapters, or even a whole book), in a series of sermons.
4. It is the aim of the leading Romanian translator to complete both the Romans and Ephesians series by his 60th birthday in 2023.
5. Murray, *The Fight of Faith*, p.158.
6. Murray, *The Fight of Faith*, p.94.
7. Murray, *The Fight of Faith*, p.226.
8. Murray, *The Fight of Faith*, p.357.
9. Murray, *The Fight of Faith*, p.360.

Winds of change

By 1954, the evangelical recovery largely led by Martyn Lloyd-Jones was gaining momentum in the English-speaking world and its mission fields abroad. Many were hopeful that this new 'reformation' would blossom into a full-blown revival. But another wind would blow from across the Atlantic to bring confusion and eventually division into the evangelical church scene.

Billy Graham and crusade evangelism
Although arguably Martyn Lloyd-Jones had the greater positive influence on evangelicalism in the twentieth century, the evangelist, Billy Graham, is much better known. William Franklin Graham Jr was born in North Carolina on 7 November 1918, four days before the First World War armistice was signed. He first professed faith in Christ nearly sixteen years later in response to an appeal to come forward during an evangelistic campaign. His exceptional preaching voice was recognized at an early stage in his life and in 1938 he offered his life to God as a preacher, promising to go and do whatever God called him to. In 1948 he married Ruth Bell, who was his faithful companion during their long life together. At first he had several preaching roles, mainly in America during the late 1940s, but became known nationwide following his 1949 crusade in Los Angeles.

Billy Graham's first major crusade in the UK lasted twelve weeks in the early spring of 1954, and was held at Haringey, North London, with the final meeting at Wembley Stadium. Because this crusade was deemed to be such a success, a further one-week crusade was held at Wembley in May 1955. Following these early crusades, Billy Graham went on to have an international ministry of crusade evangelism lasting a further fifty years.

Winds of change

This included visits to Communist countries. As Dennis Hill writes: 'The crusades went on in locations all round the world, year in and year out, sometimes as many as 25 or 30 in one year.'[1]

It has been estimated that during his lifetime Billy Graham preached to tens of millions of people (some think the figure is as high as two hundred million). A conservative estimate of the number of genuine converts is more than thirty thousand.[2]

But not all Christians have given their full endorsement to Billy Graham's crusade evangelism. Some of the major reservations are as follows:

1. Although he originally intended to work only with Bible-believing Christians, after the success of the Haringey crusade he was persuaded to cooperate with non-evangelicals. Many considered that this decision marred his future ministry.
2. For a significant number of evangelicals, the invitation system (calling people to make a physical response to the preaching), employed in all the Graham crusades, has been problematic. It was a twentieth-century re-run of the Finneyism of nineteenth-century America (see chapter 18).
3. His rather 'cosy' relationship with politicians (particularly American presidents), although well-intentioned, is certainly questionable in terms of its long-term benefits.
4. Sadly, his desire to be 'everyone's friend' led him to compromise on important aspects of the Christian faith: 'Billy Graham's views, as demonstrated by his own words, did change, often in substantial ways, as his long life proceeded.'[3]

In Billy Graham one could hardly ask for a more godly, sincere, devoted and hard-working Chistian man. Sadly, however, because his theology of conversion to Christ placed the onus on man's decision rather than the Holy Spirit's sovereign work, the majority of enquirers fell away.[4] Because of that fact, the long-term effects of his ministry on the Christian world are questionable. Billy Graham's influence on the cause of Christ in the world

A Beginner's Guide to Church History **157**

would have been much more positive had he stuck to biblical principles rather than pragmatism in both his evangelistic methods and message.

Controversy over ecumenism

The second volume of Iain Murray's biography of Martyn Lloyd-Jones has the apt title, *The Fight of Faith*. This is because Lloyd-Jones was uncompromising in his stance on essential doctrines, such as the authority of Scripture, the nature of the atonement and the doctrine of man as a sinner. His unwillingness to budge on these essentials brought him into conflict with liberals, who often vilified him. Sadly, evangelicals, too, who became willing to compromise on the ecumenical issue following the 1954 Haringey crusade, also opposed him. The ecumenical issue came to a head on 18 October 1966. On this date, at the Evangelical Alliance's request, Lloyd-Jones spoke at a public meeting in Westminster Central Hall on the question of evangelical unity. He called on his fellow evangelicals to separate themselves from the unbiblical teachings held by many in their mixed denominations, to enable them to work together in greater unity. At the end of the meeting, the chairman, John Stott,[5] publicly disagreed with Lloyd-Jones. Following Stott's lead, the majority of evangelical Anglicans, who had hitherto cooperated with evangelical nonconformists, now largely drew apart, causing an open division in the evangelical ranks. It should be added that Martyn Lloyd-Jones, though firmly biblical to the end in his own views, was always a gentleman: polite and generous to a fault, even with those who had no time for his God and Saviour.

The charismatic movement

Martyn Lloyd-Jones always had a burden for revival. He commemorated the centenary of the 1859 revival with a series of sermons on the subject in 1959. Others, too, were desirous that God would once again visit his people with reviving grace and power. A group of Anglican ministers, including David Watson and Michael Harper (a member of the

Winds of change

Westminster Fellowship), approached Lloyd-Jones in 1963 regarding their unusual 'experiences of the Holy Spirit' during all-night prayer meetings for revival. Lloyd-Jones considered that they had been 'baptized in the Holy Spirit' and encouraged them to continue praying for revival. At that stage there had been no tongues-speaking in this group. It was not until the South African Pentecostal pastor, David Du Plessis, arrived in the UK that people outside of Pentecostalism began to speak in tongues. Lloyd-Jones was unhappy about this development, which he considered was due to Du Plessis' influence and not the direct action of the Holy Spirit.[6] He was further disturbed to discover that the tongues-speaking was often psychologically-induced.[7] Interestingly, there was also at that time a turning to Reformed theology among some of the older mainstream Pentecostals.[8]

Because Lloyd-Jones considered that the work of the Holy Spirit in revival was essential to the true onward progress of the cause of Christ, he encouraged what he felt could be the beginning of a true awakening. He was also concerned at the almost anti-revival stance among some prominent evangelicals. In attempting to counteract anti-revival thinking in his preaching during the 1960s, Lloyd-Jones unwittingly provided assistance to a movement which in the end he never truly espoused.

In the latter decades of the twentieth century, the charismatic movement spread to many of the Protestant denominations and to some in Roman Catholic circles as well. In the process, many otherwise thriving evangelical churches were split, and several large groupings of charismatics emerged. Despite the mixed nature of the movement, undoubtedly some were converted out of areas of the Protestant church which had been deadened by theological liberalism. However, looking back over the last sixty years, one is forced to conclude that the movement was largely another man-made 'revival'.

Chapter 24

NOTES

1. Dennis Hill, 'Billy Graham, 1918-2018', part 2, *Evangelical Times*, June 2018.
2. Hill, 'Billy Graham', part 2.
3. David Aikman, *Billy Graham: His Life and Influence* (Nashville: Thomas Nelson, 2007), pp. 121–22.
4. Hill, 'Billy Graham', part 2.
5. John Stott was rector of All Souls Church, Langham Place, West London.
6. Iain H Murray, *D. Martyn Lloyd-Jones: the Fight of Faith* (Edinburgh: Banner of Truth Trust, 1990), p. 480.
7. Murray, *The Fight of Faith*, pp. 479–480.
8. Murray, *The Fight of Faith*, p. 481.

The church under Communism[1]

As we saw in chapter 21, in the nineteenth and early twentieth centuries the church passed through severe testing in the form of theological liberalism and Darwinian evolution. The opponents of Christianity seemed to gain great advantage over the church in the Western world from these two lines of attack, but a third major assault was to follow in the form of Communism. Although expressed in different ways, Communism is an atheistic philosophy which has shown great hostility to the church. Karl Marx, the originator of the philosophy, in his book *Das Kapital*, coined the phrase, 'Religion is the opium of the people.' Religion, in whatever form it took, must therefore be eliminated from Communist societies. Marx's dictum consequently brought Communist governments into collision with the people of God, with in many cases bloody and brutal results.

Although Marx was a German and published his book in 1867, it was not until some fifty years later, in 1917, that the first major Communist government was set up by the Soviets in Russia. Before the Revolution, evangelical churches had existed in the country for almost a hundred years. Evangelicals had migrated from Germany to the Ukraine in the 1820s, Baptists had multiplied in the Caucasus region,[2] and Bible-believing Christians had emerged among the elite in St Petersburg.[3] After full religious liberty was granted by Tsar Nicholas II in 1905, the evangelical churches were quick to capitalize on the new situation and maintained steady growth until the Revolution in 1917. Even after 1917, the evangelical churches in the Soviet Union were given comparative freedom and experienced revival during the first decade

Chapter 25

of Communist rule. This was because the Communists considered the Russian Orthodox Church to be their biggest threat, so they initially gave evangelicals greater freedom so as to draw converts away from the Orthodox Church. However, the Soviet Government's 'soft' treatment in the 1920s gave the evangelical churches a false sense of security and allowed some government agents eventually to gain influence over them. It was discovered after the fall of Communism in 1990 that nearly a third of those in the churches in Communist Eastern Europe had collaborated as informants. Even the Russian evangelical leader Ivan Prokhanov (1869–1935) was found to have cooperated with the Communist government.

As in Roman times, persecution was not continuous under the Communists, but there were periods of intense persecution directed against evangelicals.

In 1929, Stalin made a five-year plan to convert the Soviet Union into a Communist state. This included church registration (which could be denied), severe restrictions on printing religious materials, confining ministers to certain geographical areas (which limited church planting work), and forbidding meetings for children, young people, or women. A six-day week was introduced between 1929 and 1940, with one sixth of the work force off work each day. This made attending Sunday worship difficult, if not impossible. During this period, many evangelicals were arrested and sent to labour camps—an estimated twenty-two thousand to Siberia alone. When pastors were arrested, the government often closed their churches, sometimes turning church buildings into cinemas or museums. During 1944–1945, evangelical Christians, Baptists, and Pentecostals in the Soviet Union united to form one denomination, which became known as the Evangelical Christian Baptists. Although this seemed to have been the decision of the churches, the Government was definitely behind it: a centralized system of religion could be more easily and effectively infiltrated by their agents.

Persecution sometimes took the form of children being taken away from 'unfit' Christian parents and put into government-controlled orphanages. Government youth organizations were set up to indoctrinate children and young people with Communistic atheism. During this period of severe restrictions, churches limited their evangelism to personal outreach and evangelizing during weddings, funerals, and other holidays.

Communism in Eastern Europe

As the Second World War was drawing to a close, while the Western allies were advancing into Germany, Russian troops overran Eastern Europe including Poland, Czechoslovakia, Hungary, Romania, Bulgaria and the Balkan peninsula. Communist governments were set up in all these countries, which, apart from Yugoslavia and Albania, became known as the 'Eastern Bloc'. The evangelism carried out by James Stewart (see chapter 22) and others, immediately prior to the Second World War, now proved to be a great asset to believers in the Communist bloc countries. In Romania, for instance, the Romanian Baptists experienced a period of revival. Christians visiting from the West after the fall of Communism in 1990 could testify to an enhanced spiritual awareness and to large Baptist church buildings[4] being full for services which often lasted several hours.

Communism in China

The Church in China was much better prepared for the Communist takeover in 1949 than the churches in Russia had been when the 1917 Revolution occurred.

Before the crackdown of Communism, the Chinese evangelical church had learned many important lessons from foreign missionaries, not the least of which was endurance in the face of suffering. A good system of Christian education had been established (by 1906 there were fifty-eight thousand Christian schools), Bibles were readily available, and the demand for Bibles increased significantly in the years immediately before

Chapter 25

Communism. In the early 1930s, sales of entire Bibles, and especially of New Testaments, increased. This trend seemed to indicate a serious reading of the Bible which was certainly a blessed preparation for days to come when the church would be denied further copies of the Scriptures.

A key earlier event had been the Boxer Rebellion in 1900, which led to the deaths of several hundred missionaries and thousands of Chinese Christians. The witness which many Christians bore during this terrible event powerfully affected the Chinese people, and the evangelical church grew considerably right up until Communism took over in 1949. In 1925 there were still over eight thousand missionaries in China. Although they did not know the future, these missionaries had trained up thousands of national pastors and church workers, so that in 1959, when the Communists expelled all foreign workers, indigenous leaders were available to fill the gap.

Another important factor was that many pupils professed faith in Christ before they graduated from school.

During the Cultural Revolution under Mao Zedong (1966–1976), persecution became more direct and severe. All churches—even the state-controlled TSPM[5] churches—were shut down in 1966. No evangelism, public worship or even singing of hymns was allowed. Bibles and hymn books were burned. All seminaries were closed. Christians had to be careful about recognizing each other in public. Some churches would have their Sunday 'services' by means of three members meeting at one entrance to a local park and walking through the park to another entrance, where two would leave and

Mao Zedong

The church under Communism

two others would link up and so on throughout the day. This became the only 'visible' Christian fellowship still possible. Despite the severity of the government's restrictions, the unregistered 'house church' movement survived and grew. In 1982, the Chinese government officially started allowing home Bible studies, worship and prayer. Later, the massacre of students at Tiananmen Square in 1989 led to a great growth of interest in the Christian faith, especially among young people. As one person said, 'When that happened, I knew the government had lied to me.' In addition, Communists did several things which unintentionally helped the evangelical churches. They made Mandarin the standard language over the whole of China, and improved literacy and the transport system.

Over the sixteen years from 1987, when the government once more allowed Bibles to be printed in China, more than thirty million copies were produced. This greater availability of Bibles coincided with a dramatic growth of the Chinese church. By 2004 a conservative estimate of the number of true believers in China was more than sixty million. It is extremely likely that in the last eighteen years that figure has exceeded one hundred million.[6] The church in China is generally mission-minded and there are many Chinese missionaries working in minority areas of the country. There is also a strong desire to evangelize beyond China's borders in the 10/40 window.[7]

***

Russia, Eastern Europe and China were not the only countries where the church was persecuted under Communist regimes. One other notable example is Cambodia, where the fledgling church suffered particularly brutally in the killing fields of Pol Pot's Khmer Rouge.[8]

Chapter 25

NOTES

1. Much of the data for this chapter has been obtained from: John E. White, 'Growth Amidst Persecution: A Comparison of the Evangelical Church in Communist China and the Soviet Union', *International Journal of Frontier Missiology*, 29:3, Fall 2012, p. 139.
2. The Caucasus Mountains, situated between the Black Sea and the Caspian Sea, form the border between eastern Europe and western Asia.
3. Tsar Alexander I became a Bible-believing Christian in 1816.
4. During the author's visit to Cluj in Transylvania in May 1990, he was taken to the construction site for the Second Baptist Church, which would be capable of seating 1200.
5. TSPM—the Three-Self Patriotic Movement (self-governance, self-support and self-propagation) was effectively the state-controlled church, set up in 1950.
6. A retired Christian diplomat visiting China in the early twenty-first century attended a night-time baptismal service for 1300 candidates.
7. The 10/40 window is a term referring to those regions of the eastern hemisphere, plus the European and African part of the western hemisphere, located between 10 and 40 degrees north of the equator, a general area that has least access to the Christian message and Christian resources.
8. Don Cormack, *Killing Fields, Living Fields* (Sevenoaks: OMF Publishing, 2009).

New model, new ministries

During the nineteenth century, most of the European nations had colonies in other parts of the world. This colonization is now recognized as morally dubious because it unfairly exploited the natural resources of the undeveloped world. It made Europe rich and rarely recompensed the countries whose resources were being used. On the other hand, this colonial period proved to be of great assistance to the advance of the gospel. Christian missionaries were able to move relatively freely from Europe to other parts of the world and plant churches far and wide. This situation changed as the twentieth century progressed, as the European 'empires' one by one disintegrated and eventually disappeared completely. The British Commonwealth is a loose association of those nations which had once been part of the British Empire. With former European colonies becoming independent, the colonial model for world mission was fast becoming obsolete.

When Communism took over in China and other parts of the Far East, foreign missionaries were expelled, or they realized that it was too dangerous to remain. At first this came as a great disappointment to mission workers, but in the providence of God it proved to be a blessing in disguise. Young churches in many areas were forced to stand on their own feet, and many missionaries were thrust out into other parts of the 'harvest field'.[1] As we noted in the last chapter, the church in China grew under Communism beyond all expectations. Other smaller people-groups could now receive attention from those bringing the Christian message for the first time.

New ministries

Towards the end of the twentieth century, a new approach emerged for Christian ministry around the world. Its primary feature was to support

Chapter 26

existing churches by means of training for pastors and church workers. The availability of relatively low-cost air travel has made it possible for European and American pastors to make short visits to countries such as Burma, Pakistan and Zimbabwe (to name but three). A journey which a hundred years ago would have taken a few months can now be achieved in under twenty-four hours. These overseas visits are often by a small team of pastors to a group of churches. Visas can usually be obtained for such short visits even where 'missionary' visas are not available, although they have sometimes been refused. In the 1990s, one pastor who had been with a team on several very successful evangelistic tours to Hindu villages was refused entry to India and has not been able to return since. Other pastors have been able to return year after year for as long as a decade. The churches have been very appreciative of this kind of help and have often arranged very full schedules for the visitors so as to maximize their usefulness.

Pastors' conferences, such as the African Pastors' Conferences in southern Africa and the annual conference organized by Cubao Reformed Baptist Church in Manila, have also been useful.

There have also been a number of instances of individuals relocating to other parts of the world to plant churches, set up ministerial training colleges and centres and engage in educational and relief ministries. Often these missionaries have been supported by a few churches in the West. Some have married local believers and been able to stay in their foreign location for decades. Still others have engaged in translation of Christian literature into local languages, and hundreds of titles have been published in this way. (Bible translation has, of course, been an ongoing priority everywhere.)

Radio and TV ministries have been established in many areas; not just for evangelism, but also to support and train pastors and other church workers. One example of this is Grace Baptist Mission's *Serving Today* radio programme, which is aired for the benefit of English-speaking church leaders in Africa and India. From time to time, GBM staff have visited recipients of the programmes who have corresponded with the mission centre in Abingdon. The Middle East Reformed Fellowship (MERF) has established training centres in Cyprus, Egypt, Lebanon, northern Kenya, Ethiopia and Indonesia. They also broadcast evangelistic programmes in several languages. SAT-7 has a TV ministry to much of the Muslim world.

The growth of the churches being supported by these ministries may at times seem slow, but they are generally, at the time of writing, moving in a positive direction.

Persecution

With the church expanding all over the world (apart from the West), it is not surprising that persecution has increased. The leaders of all other ideologies and religions, once they realize what the Christian gospel is about, will inevitably persecute the people of God. Today, persecution is most severe in Communist North Korea, much of the Islamic world, and where Hinduism and Buddhism are the majority religions. Persecution from the Roman Catholic and Eastern Orthodox churches is far more muted than in previous times, although it has not disappeared completely.[2]

During the last decade, a new threat from militant secularism has arisen in Europe and the USA. Over the past fifty years, Western society has progressively abandoned the values on which our whole culture was established. Modern 'values' such as gay rights and transgender issues are being promoted as being more important than many traditional principles of Christian origin. As a result of this huge shift in 'morality', Christians are being taken to court or losing their jobs for remaining faithful to their biblical principles. Organizations such as the Christian Institute have been set up to oppose such attacks on Christians and Christian values.

NOTES

1 Luke 10:2.
2 A Romanian evangelical organization has recently commented on its website: 'The Romanian Orthodox Church is a virulently anti-Evangelical organization.'

Conclusion

And so our tale is nearly told. Our overview of the Christian era is almost up to date. It has not been comprehensive but has focused on most of the main features of the history of the people of God down the centuries.

The church of Jesus Christ began its life around AD 27 in Jerusalem with three thousand baptized on the day of Pentecost. Its journey through these two thousand years has not been without its 'many dangers, toils and snares'. At first the church's great enemy, the devil, tried the all-out frontal assault of persecution under the Romans. They had to retire from the field when the number of believers had reached several million (approximately 10% of the empire). Early heresies were fought off, too, when God raised up champions to defend the cause of truth. Then came the insidious stranglehold of medieval Christendom (both Roman Catholic and Eastern Orthodox), which slowly tried to squeeze the life out of the professing church, and which suppressed, often brutally at times, any attempt to return to a purer and more biblically-based faith.

But the word of God cannot be chained (2 Tim. 2:9), and will always prevail. The light of the gospel shone out again with amazing brilliance, first from Wittenberg and then from Geneva. The church became again like the great army, brought back from the dead, in Ezekiel 37. Initially this awakening provoked outward opposition from the corrupt medieval religious authorities, and later there were more subtle attacks, on the reliability of the Bible and its core teachings, from within the church's own ranks. Yet despite this opposition, the great impetus generated by the Reformation and Puritan eras and subsequent revivals issued in the modern worldwide missionary movement. So much so, that there is today no major country in the world where there are not Bible-believing

Conclusion

Christians, sometimes in significant numbers.[1] This is true under even the most repressive regimes, whether Islamic or Communist.

But perhaps the most significant area of unfinished business for the church today concerns the people-groups who have never heard the Christian message. Thankfully, agencies such as the New Tribes Mission (now known as Ethnos 360) are still actively working among such people—bringing them the gospel and translating the Scriptures for them.

The call, then, which comes from this brief look at the cause of Christ down the ages, is for all who are in gospel work (particularly on the front line), to 'keep on keeping on', so that we may soon hear 'the cry of the archangel and the trumpet call of God'. As the hymn puts it:

He comes, whose advent trumpet drowns the last of time's evangels,
Emmanuel crowned with many crowns, the Lord of saints and angels.[2]

Amen, so be it. 'Even so, come, Lord Jesus!' (Rev. 22:20, AV).

Soli Deo gloria.

NOTES

1 For example, there are 7000 believers in modern-day Turkey and 30,000 in modern-day Israel.
2 'For My sake and the Gospel's, go' by Edward Henry Bickersteth.

Bibliography

J. A. Wylie, *History of Protestantism*, Vols 1–3

S. M. Houghton, *Sketches from Church History*, Banner of Truth Trust, 1980.

J. Gresham Machen, *The New Testament, An Introduction to its Literature and History*, Banner of Truth Trust, 1990.

Philip Schaff, *The History of the Christian Church*, Vols 1 & 2

Iain Murray, *The Forgotten Spurgeon*, Banner of Truth Trust, 1966.

William Cunningham, *Historical Theology*, Vol. 1, Banner of Truth Trust, 1960.

Merle D'Aubigné, *The Reformation in England*, Vols 1 & 2, Banner of Truth Trust, 1962.

Nick Needham, *2000 Years of Christ's Power*, Vol. 2, Grace Publications, 2016

C. P. Hallihan, *The Protestant Reformation*, Trinitarian Bible Society, 2017.

Cyril J. Davey, *The Monk Who Shook the World*, Lutterworth Press, 2000.

E. M. Johnson, *Man of Geneva*, Banner of Truth, 1977.

Brian Edwards, *God's Outlaw*, Evangelical Press.

Colin Hamer, *Anne Boleyn*, Day One Publications, 2017.

Arnold Dallimore, *George Whitefield*, Vol. 1, Banner of Truth Trust, 1970.

Bibliography

Timothy George, *Faithful Witness*, IVP, 1991

Iain Murray, *Revival and Revivalism*, Banner of Truth Trust, 1994

John Simpson, *Modern Revivals: Their Features and Incidents* (London 1862)

C. H. Spurgeon, *New Park Street Pulpit 1860*, Banner of Truth Trust

Ruth Tucker, *From Jerusalem to Irian Jaya: A Biographical History of Christian Missions*, Zondervan, 1983.

John McDonald, *Grace to the Nations*, Grace Baptist Mission, 2011.

Terry A. Chrisope, *Towards a Sure Faith*, Christian Focus Publications, 2000.

Nathaniel Jeanson, *Replacing Darwin, the new origin of species*, Answers in Genesis, 2018.

J. C. Ryle, *Expository Thoughts on John*, Evangelical Press, 1977.

Iain H Murray, *D. Martyn Lloyd-Jones*, Vol. 1, Banner of Truth Trust, 1982.

Bethan Lloyd-Jones, *Memories of Sandfields*, Banner of Truth Trust, 2008.

Iain H Murray, *The Fight of Faith*, Banner of Truth Trust, 1982.

Dennis Hill, *Billy Graham, 1918–2018, Part 2*, Evangelical Times, June 2018.

David Aikman, *Billy Graham: His Life and Influence*, Thomas Nelson, 2007.

Growth Amidst Persecution: A Comparison of the Evangelical Church in Communist China and the Soviet Union, John E. White, International Journal of Frontier Missiology, 29:3, Fall 2012.

Don Cormack, *Killing Fields, Living Fields*, Monarch Publications, 1997.

Serving Today

About Serving Today

(The author, Philip Parsons, has been a regular contributor to the Serving Today radio programme and we are very pleased that this book is also being adapted for radio.)

- In production since 2002 by the Radio Department of Grace Baptist Mission (CIO).
- A radio programme dedicated to supporting pastors and church leaders, mainly in developing countries.
- Over 700 programmes produced to date, Serving Today provides guides to preaching from various Bible books, help with pastoral issues, doctrine overviews, biblical perspectives on topical matters.
- Can be heard through TWR-Africa and other local stations across Africa, and via the internet (go to www.gbm.org.uk/radio)
- 'The Serving Today broadcasts are the only ones I know of that are specifically directed at pastors. It teaches pastors how to construct a sermon and also gives advice and guidance when dealing with a congregation.' (as described by TWR-Africa)
- Also available to individual pastors and church leaders in the following ways:

  on CD (MP3 format) together with a copy of the follow-up booklet sent by post as each series is completed. (This option is specifically for the support of those with limited access to resources.)

  by weekly email as an MP3 attachment

  To receive Serving Today in either of these ways, please contact us at the address below.

Serving Today
GBM Radio
12 Abbey Close
Abingdon
Oxfordshire OX14 3JD (UK)

Email: radio@gbm.org.uk
Web: www.gbm.org.uk/radio

Twitter: @ServingTodayGBM

- Please pray for the ministry.